NEVER MAKE A RESERVATION IN YOUR OWN NAME

Never Make a Reservation in Your Own Name

And other intriguing ideas for travelers

Leonard S. Bernstein

Rand McNally & Company

Chicago • New York • San Francisco

"Remembrance of Things Pasta," and "Beware of Aero!" appeared originally in *TWA Ambassador* magazine. "The French Connection" appeared in the *Saturday Evening Post*, reprinted by permission. "Your Friends Took 300 Slides of London—Do You Really Want to See Them?" is reprinted by permission of *House Beautiful*, copyright 1972, The Hearst Corporation. "Surviving the French Maître d' " appeared originally in the *New York Times*, reprinted by permission. "How to Make a Million Dollars on Your Vacation" is reprinted with permission of *Holiday* magazine.

Quotation from "The Road Not Taken," by Robert Frost, from *The Poetry of Robert Frost* edited by Edward Connery Lathem. Copyright 1916, © 1969 by Holt, Rinehart and Winston. Copyright 1944 by Robert Frost. Reprinted by permission of Holt, Rinehart and Winston, Publishers.

Cover and text illustrations by John Huehnergarth.

Library of Congress Cataloging in Publication Data

Bernstein, Leonard S.
  Never make a reservation in your own name and
other intriguing ideas for travelers.

  1. Travel. I. Title.
G151.B49   910'.2'02   81-1752
ISBN 0-528-81113-4   AACR2

For my mother, with love.

Contents

Introduction

There are, really, only two kinds of travelers: those who visit the Eiffel Tower and love it, and those who find it boring. Hundreds, maybe thousands of travel books have been written for those who love it. Nothing has been written for those who find it boring.

That's too bad. I'd guess there are thousands of people—not oddballs, not jet-setters—who are tired of seeing the ruins of ancient cities and would rather get into a volleyball game in Paris, go to a meat-pie tasting in London, or speak Italian to some stranger on the Ponte Vecchio in Florence.

I'm a traveler. Not an around-the-world traveler or a sophisticated professional traveler, but just a plain old two-weeks-in-Portugal-during-my-summer-vacation traveler. Over the years I've discovered that I'm not delighted with a number of the sights and sounds that I'm supposed to be delighted by. I've found out that I don't like to carry a camera, don't like to take photographs, don't like to ride tour buses, and don't like most tour guides.

What *do* I like? Well, tell me about some dinky restaurant in Paris, where Mama serves up a marvelous Cassoulet, and I'll be there. Through rain or snow, through the worst part of town, through language barrier or insult, I'll be there.

And if there's a tennis game in town—even at a private club, even if nobody speaks English—I'm going to try to play. To which a reasonable person might say, "You don't have to travel to Lisbon to play tennis." It's true, but I *like* to play tennis in Lisbon.

And I like to speak a little of the language, so I have a homemade language course that I follow before I leave. It sounds like work, but it's not; it's fun. And there are a lot of surprises when you can speak the language in a foreign country.

You can't do without Fielding or Michelin, but they don't tell you everything. Michelin may name the three-star restaurants, but what do you do if you are strolling around town, and it's one o'clock in the afternoon, and you're suddenly famished? Your Michelin is back at the hotel, and even if you had it you don't feel like going crosstown for lunch. You like this part of town and you want to stay here, but where do you find a respectable Coq au Vin? Here's what you do: You walk into the nearest wine, cheese, or pastry shop and sooner or later you strike up a modest conversation, even in halting French, with the proprietor. Before long you feel comfortable asking him if he could recommend a small family restaurant in the vicinity.

Invariably, around the corner, Mama is serving a Coq au Vin that even Michelin hasn't discovered yet, so you walk right in and say that Monsieur Derain, at the wineshop, thought you might enjoy lunch there. *Voilà*! You are a member of the family. And to be a member of the family is to dine very well indeed. So that if you order a '71 Bordeaux, and the '70 is better for the same price, Mama brings out the '70. And if you order the peach tart for dessert, but Mama thinks you ought to have at least a stab at the chocolate mousse, well then there will be a corner of mousse on your plate—and a couple of fresh raspberries.

What an enormous difference that makes. I've been to Tour d'Argent and Taillevent in Paris, and to the good smaller restaurants as well. They can be spectacular, but they can also be stiff, and I'm never quite sure that I'm not the Ugly American. The difference is to be welcome.

So in these pages can be found assorted ideas, schemes, and adventures—reliable and unreliable—to make your trip more exciting. Nothing is guaranteed. No discount tickets are included. No sound advice is offered on how to save a buck. Most of the stories and most of the suggestions are way-out, impractical, even outrageous. But none of them hurt. I think you might try a couple.

I shall be telling this with a sigh
Somewhere ages and ages hence:
Two roads diverged in a wood, and I–
I took the one less traveled by,
And that has made all the difference.
                              Robert Frost

Thirty Days to Learning Italian

Everyone has his own insanities about traveling. Some want to see fourteen countries in three days, and some want to see three countries in fourteen days. One person carries four cameras; another carries three restaurant guides. Some say the Louvre is a must, while others miss it on purpose.

I point this out to excuse my own peculiarity: I won't visit a country unless I've learned the language.

Before you say, "Isn't that terribly difficult?" let me tell you how it can be done. It's not difficult at all, and it can be exciting.

First, it is not necessary to be fluent in a language. You are going to be in the country for only two or three weeks. I try to get to the point where I can always be understood, and can understand most of what is said to me if it is said slowly. I follow two steps. First, I buy a Berlitz Self-Teacher Book, which has about forty lessons. Second, I find a tutor.

I devote an hour a night to the lessons and finish them in about a month. Some people might prefer a tutor at the beginning, but I find that a mistake. When you don't know the word for "book," a tutor only slows you down. You simply don't need a tutor to build basic vocabulary. True, you will be more certain of learning correct pronunciation at the start, but I have never found that a serious problem. The Berlitz book does an excellent job of sounding out the word, and you can refine your pronunciation later.

There is also the question of language records. I've tried them and I don't think they work. If you don't know a language, and you listen to it spoken on a record, when the record is over you still don't know the language. It's a little like trying to learn spelling before you have studied the sounds of the individual letters. Or it might also be like trying to build a structure starting with the second floor. The cornerstone of understanding a language is building a basic vocabulary. Tutors and records come afterward.

Possibly some very qualified language teachers will not agree with me. Some will say that a crash course at a language school is the best way. Others will point to records or to their own professional system. I'm sure their systems work, but they don't work for me. I don't want to spend two nights a week at a language school, traveling there and back, and spending a considerable amount of money. I'd rather get home for dinner and pull out the language book whenever a free hour appears. To each his own.

It is also true that I am not learning a language to engage in international diplomacy; I'm learning it to have some fun. I'm not likely to use it after the trip, and I'm willing to invest only so much money and energy in the learning process.

So I have now invested thirty hours and $7.95 for the book, and I have a basic vocabulary of some 500 words. That might seem like a lot, but it is surprising how much of a language you know before you even begin to study it. Consider Spanish: You already know *adiós* and *buenos dias*, *señor* and *señorita*. You know *sombrero* means "hat," and as soon as you see *restaurante* you recognize it. *Reservación* is easy, so there you are; you probably already know enough Spanish to negotiate your way through a lovely dinner of Arroz con Pollo with *vino blanco*.

After the forty lessons you can speak in the present tense and perhaps handle a few important verbs in the past and future. Actually, I treat the past and future rather lightly and never learn them well. This is because I use the present tense about 90% of the time, including some of the time when I should be using the past. Learning to conjugate every verb in all three tenses is an energy drain without sufficient reward. I'm not trying to impress anyone with my fluidity—and in fact I never have. I just want to be able to walk into a small shop off the tourist route and be able to communicate.

I do learn the past and future tenses of the important verbs. The fact is, you use the verbs "to have," "to want," and "to be" about as often as all the other verbs combined. Half the trick of learning a language is learning what not to learn.

I have my own approach to verbs and it saves me hours of work. The purists may frown, but I have a specific objective: to be able to handle as much of a language as I can in a very short time. So I concentrate on verb *infinitives*. I do not learn their conjugations. Aside from six or seven of the most common verbs, the only verb I learn to conjugate is "to want." For example, in Spanish, I learn to conjugate *querer*. I learn to say, "I want," "he wants," "I would like"—perhaps six applications. Then I learn the verb infinitives: "to go," "to see," "to order," "to buy," "to pay." When I enter a store or a restaurant and am asked what I would like, I always say, "I want to buy," or "I want to order." When I enter a cab I *don't* say, "Please take me to . . ." I say, "I want to go." In this way I can learn fifty verbs and use fifty verbs instead of learning fifty verbs in a billion tenses, which I never get right anyway.

I also choose carefully the words I learn. I never learn the word for "closet," "wall," or "floor." But I learn "soap" and "towel." I learn all the restaurant words—"glass," "knife," "wine," "check" —because I spend a lot of time in restaurants. I never learn the names of flowers or animals because I never use them. I was in Portugal recently for two weeks and there were magnificent flowers blooming all over the place, and I never used a flower name once.

If flowers are your hobby and you buy your food in Portuguese supermarkets (alas, there are some), learn the flower names and skip the food names. The principle is the same: Learn what you will use.

After an hour a night for one month (that's not too bad, is it?), you will be amazed at how much you know. Now you get a tutor. I call International House in New York City, which is the residence for 500 foreign students, most of them attending Columbia. If I lived in Detroit or Los Angeles, I would call a university. There have to be people fluent in any language at a university. At International House, most of the students are delighted to give lessons in their language and earn some money. They charge $7 or $8 an hour and they will come to your office or home. I spend two hours a week, mostly in simple conversation. When the tutor uses a word that is not in my vocabulary (often enough), I just jot it down and learn it later. I need the tutor's time for talk. I don't want him to say, "The word for book is *libro*. Now repeat after me."

The evening before I leave for the country I try to spend three straight hours with the tutor—perhaps at dinner, or walking around the city. We only speak his language.

Understand that 10% of the words he uses I will miss, but I can still follow him. Now and then I have to ask him to repeat slowly what he has just said. All in all, it works.

The best part is that you are not only learning a language from the tutor but learning about the country. In addition, you are finding out how a foreigner sees New York. The chances are that you are also making a friend. I still correspond with Luciano Stecca, who taught me Italian three years ago. It was exciting just being with him, a bright, informed student at Columbia. I would have been delighted to spend every hour I did with him without learning his language.

But Luciano was going to be sure that I learned it. We spent my last evening in New York at a Chinese restaurant (a new experience for Luciano) and spoke Italian for three hours. When I got on the plane the next day, I was ready.

I was ready with Italian and I also had an invitation to visit Luciano's uncle, who owned a leather goods shop in Rome. And I had two great family restaurant recommendations, and instructions to try some dishes that are not on the menus of Italian restaurants in New York.

The restaurants in a city are the best reason to speak the language. You are free to go anywhere. The restaurants I enjoy most are those where they do not speak English at all and where I do not meet the Great Neck P.T.A. The "classy" restaurants are very good, of course, but they are not the spirit of the city. And even if I go to a "classy" restaurant for dinner, I prefer a dinky little joint for lunch.

One thing about dinky little joints. In Italy they serve great food. There are no "luncheonettes" in Italy and there are no Howard Johnsons. In the dinky little restaurants, Mama stands behind that stove and turns out an Osso Buco that is delicious.

My wife, Rita, and I landed in Rome, unpacked, and headed to a Mama restaurant for lunch. I was nervous but it didn't last long. When Mama heard that I could handle a little Italian she gave me a big hug, and three other waiters came over, smiling, to say hello. (Just like New York.)

One of the waiters spoke some English and tried to help me when I got stuck. Mama wouldn't hear of it. "In Italy you speak Italian," she said. "We will understand you." She certainly understood what we wanted for lunch. It was sensational.

I found out quickly that a language is very elastic. There are five ways of saying everything. For example, when you are finished with lunch and can't say, "I am finished," you can say, "Enough," or "No more." You will find the vocabulary that you own adapts to most situations.

Of course, a restaurant is only one place where you will enjoy being able to negotiate the language. You can stay at a hotel that does not cater only to American tourists—a much less expensive hotel (but just as nice) that has Italians to talk to instead of your bridge crowd.

The next day we visited Luciano's uncle. The Italians are very warm to begin with, but when you bring news of a nephew from New York City, you are part of the family.

It was my second day of speaking Italian and I was improving. I discovered that one of the best ways to use and practice the language was to take cabs. You have a captive audience. It's not exactly easy to walk up to someone at your hotel (although it can be done) and start talking Italian, but in a cab it is perfectly natural to ask the driver, "Do you live in Rome?" or, "What is the name of that building?" I often took cabs just to see the city and speak the language.

We left Rome after five days and drove to Florence, where I had a most exciting and also my most painful experience with the Italian language.

I have loved the painting of the Italian Renaissance ever since college. In particular I love the frescoes of Masaccio and Piero della Francesca. There are hardly any examples of their work in New York.

The greatest work of Masaccio is a series of frescoes in the Brancacci Chapel of the Carmine, a small church in a rather tucked-away part of the city of Florence. It is certainly among the dozen greatest works of the fifteenth century.

We arrived at the church. The frescoes were magnificent. But there was nobody there to answer questions or explain the significance of the work. I scurried off to find someone to help and I did finally find a monk in some odd corner of the church who could talk to us about the Masaccio, but he didn't speak a word of English.

I begged him to try in Italian, and he agreed. The subtleties of early Italian fresco painting are difficult to understand even if you do understand the language, and I was struggling. But the monk realized how anxious we were to learn about the frescoes, and of course the frescoes were the pride of his church. He spoke very slowly and explained every corner of the work. And I understood most of it.

But all things didn't go as well as that. The following night I was wide awake at eleven and I left our hotel room and walked a few blocks to the Ponte Vecchio, the great old bridge of Florence.

The bridge is a meeting place, or simply a cool spot where the people of Florence stand around, smoke, watch the river Arno, and consider perhaps that the armies of Caesar watched the same river long before life became as complicated as it is now.

I was standing on the bridge and a fellow asked me in Italian for a cigarette. I asked him if he lived in Florence, and he asked me if I was American. An hour later we were still talking. I was terribly excited that I could maintain a reasonably intelligent conversation. I knew that I was missing words and certainly inferences and emphases, but that didn't bother me at all. It seemed to me that this was everything I had studied for.

He asked if I would like to walk and have him point out some of the old buildings. Absolutely. There seemed to be no danger. The streets were active. He was a student at the university. And one just doesn't worry about getting mugged in Florence.

We walked through the city and talked. He was very friendly and very tolerant of my limitations with the language.

And then, almost imperceptibly, the conversation shifted gears. We were talking about friends and friendships, and I had only a fuzzy idea of what was being said. I tried to hang on, often nodding understanding when I didn't understand, figuring I would pick up the thread. As I nodded he went on, but after a few minutes I was lost. He was saying something and I was just losing too much of it.

"I'm sorry," I said, "I just don't understand."

He looked at me painfully, forced by my limitations to come right out in the open.

"*Amore*," he said, "*amore*."

I understood at once. While I had dabbled in my pleasant language game, tactlessly driving into the private corners of his life, I had led him to believe that I was interested.

"I'm sorry," I said, "my wife is at the hotel and I should be returning."

He looked at me, a little confused and a little hurt, but finally he smiled and reached out to shake my hand.

"Good night, I hope you continue to enjoy my city."

I walked back to the hotel. There wasn't much that I could have done about it. In my exuberance the conversation had gone way over my head.

It is wise to know this can happen. You can order dinner, bargain for prices, talk about New York, learn about a city, but there are some things you cannot do.

It didn't discourage me, and the next morning I was chatting with the chambermaid, questioning the hotel bill, and ordering espresso at a sidewalk café.

The city of Florence is one of the grand cities of the world. It's a joy to be there, to walk the streets, to see the buildings a thousand years old, to buy an apple. And if you can speak their language you are so free; you are so exhilarated. You become a citizen of the world.

Please try it—just once. It will not cost you very much and I promise that you will experience a different kind of trip. I suspect that afterward you will not visit a country any other way.

The French Connection

I will admit that people often have some good ideas why you *shouldn't* learn a language:

1. It takes a lot of time.
2. English is spoken in most European countries.
3. You will use the language for only two weeks.

Furthermore, it's true that the taxi drivers in Lisbon will overcharge you whether you speak Portuguese or not. And fluent French won't save you a franc in the $50-a-head restaurants of Paris.

Certainly you can get by without knowing the language, but there is one more terrific reason for learning it: Consider who you might find to teach you.

Two years ago we decided to spend our summer vacation in France. I thought it would be helpful to know a few French words, so I called International House in New York City.

"I'd like to hire a tutor in French. Are there any available?"

"Would you like a male or female tutor?"

"Well, I don't know. I hadn't given that any thought."

"O.K. then, we will send you whoever is available. Now where would you like your lessons?"

"Is it possible to get a tutor to come to my office?"

"Oh, yes. Our tutors will give you lessons anywhere you like."

"Well then, my office—tomorrow at five."

"Fine, a tutor will call you before then to confirm. Good-bye."

I put down the phone and thought about what I had just arranged. How could I have bungled that question about male or

female? A female French tutor! I could flunk the course and I wouldn't mind. I picked up the phone.

"Listen, I think I just spoke to you about a tutor in French. Well, you see, my wife might want to take lessons with me and she would feel more comfortable with a woman. So do you think you could arrange . . ."

(Last year International House received 267 calls from men who wanted language lessons, and 243 thought their wives might want to take lessons with them.)

"Let me see who is available," she said. "Ah, yes, you will receive a call from Monique."

Monique! I could picture her right away. Five-foot seven, 115 pounds. I can't tell you the rest.

The balance of the day was wasted. Business associates came in for important decisions. I told them to see me later in the week. The phone rang; I grabbed for the receiver.

"Phone call for you, Mr. Bernstein—from Mr. Brody."

Damn it!

"Listen, Susan, if I get a call from someone named Monique, don't lose it. Yes, Susan, that's Monique. M-O-N-I-Q-U-E. How come all of a sudden you need the spelling?"

At 4:30 that afternoon the call came.

"Ah, Meestaire Bernstein, I weel come to see you tomorrow at five. I bring all my things weeth me . . ."

"What things? What things?"

"Oh, my lesson books and notes, but we won't work too much from zee books. Eet weel be very informal. The fee is $7—for everything."

"For everything?"

"Yes, ees that O.K.?"

"Oh, sure, certainly."

I couldn't even read the paper on the train home, and when I got in the house Rita asked at once what was wrong. Of course I didn't tell her. No sense busting up my marriage until I at least got a few lessons in.

At five o'clock the next day Monique arrived at the office. Descriptions will do no good. She was simply, in every way, an extraordinary woman.

"I come to see Meestaire Bernstein," she said.

I took her into my office. She was olive-toned and dark-eyed, articulate and charming. I fell in love with her immediately.

It was evening. The light outside had softened just a little. There was that sense of quiet that sets in near day's end. She crossed her legs.

"We begin weeth lesson one. The word for book is *livre*. Eet must come from deep in your throat, and you must move your lips like thees."

Visions of life abroad danced through my head. The capitals of Europe, St. Tropez and Cannes, the small secluded villages of Italy.

"You are not concentrating."

"I'm trying," I said truthfully.

The executive staff pleaded with the receptionist to find out when Monique was returning for lesson two. They were lined up in the reception area trying to act discreet.

I did my best to avoid distractions, but Monique sensed that my attention was not riveted to vocabulary. Toward the end of the lesson she made a suggestion.

"Sometimes eet ees bettaire to have a lesson out of the office where eet ees more relaxing. Perhaps at some petite French restaurant where we can recite the menu."

That was it. I knew it. My heart started pounding. If I messed this up I deserved nothing ever again out of life.

And so lesson three was arranged for a small French restaurant. I told Rita about my sick friend in Columbia Presbyterian, got a sunlamp treatment from the barber, and met her at seven. She looked spectacular.

I have to interrupt this to point out that I was, through all of this, learning French. I mean, there are probably some pretty concerned people reading this, and I want you to know that this started out as an argument for learning a foreign language—and that's what it is. Whatever else it is, is extra.

We ordered a bottle of Chambertin, and smiled warmly at each other. Monique reached into her bag. A present for me, no doubt. It was our French lesson book.

"We begin lesson three. Repeat after me."

"For godsakes, Monique, not so loud. I thought we might . . . you know . . . just talk."

Monique opened her incredibly beautiful doe eyes and watched me for a moment. I had indiscretion written all over me. French girls learn how to handle this at age seven.

"Meestaire Bernstein, repeat after me, *Caneton à l'Orange, Boeuf Bourguignonne.*"

All right, so I didn't sweep Monique off her feet. You have something better to do than learn French from a gorgeous Parisienne? I had ten lessons with Monique and I learned a lot, even if it wasn't all about the language.

The following year Rita and I decided to visit Portugal.

Friends said, "You're not going to learn Portuguese, are you? That's a terribly difficult language."

Perhaps it is, but that has nothing to do with it. I wouldn't mind taking Sanskrit if someone like Monique was teaching it.

I called International House. Visions of a Portuguese Monique ignited my imagination. "Hello, International House? I would like to take lessons in Portuguese. Could you have the young lady at my office tomorrow? You can't—why not? There is only one Portuguese student at International House? His name is Fernando?"

So I caution you to research your country beyond the limits of Fielding and Fodor. All the countries are fun to visit and all the languages are fun to learn. But all the teachers are not as much fun as Monique. Which is not to say that I didn't learn Portuguese from Fernando. My concentration, in fact, improved remarkably.

If you're considering France this summer, think about Monique. She is still at International House.

How do I know? Must you ask me *everything*?

Surviving the French Maître d'

Possibly there is one place you should avoid if you have bothered to learn French before your visit to France—and that is the three-star Paris restaurant. All over the world, maître d's appreciate your learning their language. In Paris they glare at you.

Actually, they glare at you in Paris whether you speak French or not, and their glare seems to say:

"This is my restaurant. What are you doing here?"

"You are American, aren't you? I can tell by the way you dress."

"You aren't going to try out your high school French on me, are you?"

Now here I am, and I've been spending the last month or so learning a language. Last year, when I learned Italian, I got hugged by twelve waiters and was pronounced the blood brother of at least seven maître d's. So naturally, here in Paris, I expect a little smile—a handshake, maybe.

No chance; the French maître d' is out to make you miserable, and I would be miserable, still, except that one day, out of the depths of humiliation and despair, I came upon the System.

I want to say that the French maître d' is no worse than the New York maître d'. I hate them both. The only difference is you don't need a system to get along in New York. Only lots of courage.

The reason you need a system in Paris is that the homemade language course doesn't always work. It works in the smaller restaurants and it works in the grand restaurants outside of Paris. But in the elegant establishments of Paris it doesn't work. Nothing works. That's too bad, because I had studied hard. I could pronounce the French wines like Château Ducru-Beaucaillou, and I knew what Agneau à la Mode du Bercy was. I understood the menu, felt I could pronounce the dishes properly in French, and was prepared to try. As I've said before, you *can* get by in English, but dinner is much more enjoyable if you can manage it in French.

The problem is, if you approach a French maître d' and speak anything less than fluent French, you get ripped apart.

I would enter a restaurant, and say in very mediocre French, "I called for a reservation at two o'clock. My name is . . ."

And he would interrupt with that exasperated look and say, "It would be much better if you spoke English. We all understand English here."

In two fast sentences, the French maître d' makes you feel like an idiot for trying his language and destroys whatever minimal confidence you had in trying to handle the menu in French. Not only that, but he has now established that intimidating one-upmanship that I thought I had left behind in New York.

Being intimidated is the worst way to start a lunch in France or anywhere else. You are afraid to ask questions. The waiter suggests the *plat du jour* and you hesitate in asking him what else he recommends. If you ask him in English, it's a sure thing that he doesn't understand English and races away to get the maître d'. If you ask him in French, he rattles off three alternatives in Grand Prix French, and you miss the whole thing. Lunch becomes a contest. Are you to be served comfortably and graciously, or are you imposing on the waiter's time?

But what are you going to do? You are in a strange country with different customs. It is a new language and, for the most part, a strange menu.

In Lisbon, if you try Portuguese, they seem honored. No hugs and kisses, but lots of patience. And if you need help, they give you the missing word and then allow you to continue in Portuguese. Maître d's have come to my table to take the order, and, recognizing that I was American (how can they tell?), addressed me in English. And as soon as I spoke the first simple sentence in Portuguese, there was not another English word until I got stuck (which was soon enough).

Not the French.

The System? Well, it became apparent in Paris that I was going to be intimidated in either French or English, and so, after three or four days I stopped caring and walked into a restaurant and said in English that I had a two o'clock reservation.

And because I didn't care, I guess I said it with a very rapid Brooklyn accent. The maître d' was perplexed; he didn't understand. I missed his confusion, of course, being certain that his expression was just another weapon in the arsenal. So I said it again, the same way, and he still didn't understand.

"I'm terribly sorry," he said, "but I did not understand what you said. Could you kindly repeat it?" He took a step back, and smiled politely.

So I repeated it in French. The same awful French I always use.

And he said, "Why, you speak French, and so very well. Yes, we have your reservation, Mr. Bernstein. Perhaps you would like that table near the window."

When the waiter came to take the order I zipped off two sentences in such rapid New York dialect that for a moment he could only stare at me blankly. He didn't even know if it was English. When he recovered and turned to get the maître d', I said in French, "Perhaps we could try in French if you will speak very slowly." He smiled, the rat, and we proceeded in French.

I asked him all kinds of questions and looked him right in the eye. One false move and I would have sprung out a sentence in English. He knew it.

The main thing was that I was comfortable. In that fine balance that exists between the served and the server, the control had shifted to my side. The System was working.

It wasn't really a system yet, but it got to be one very quickly.

Instead of walking into a restaurant torn with discomfort about the first exchange with the maître d', I walked in with my head up. If the maître d' looked particularly imperious I gunned him down with a short blast. More often I felt confident enough to begin in French. If he started in with, "Really, we all speak English here," I shifted to English, and he found out that they all didn't speak English there.

If he was really arrogant, the conversation went like this:

(In French) "Good afternoon, I have a reservation for lunch at two o'clock."

(In English) "Really, you might try English. We all speak English here."

(In English) "CertainlylistenIcalledinatwoo'clocklunchreservation."

(In English) "I'm very sorry, but I think I missed what you said."

"CertainlylistenIcalledina . . ." Rattled off faster than before, or backward.

"Pardon, Monsieur, I am terribly sorry, but I do not understand."

And then, in French, with a smile, "Good afternoon, I have a reservation for lunch at two o'clock."

"Ah, Monsieur, *très bien, très bien.*"

So there you have it. The most important thing you have to know when dining in Paris.

If you know the System you will probably never have to use it. It's like karate. Knowing it is all that matters.

The Pastry Principle

Take this test: You are approaching a small restaurant on the Left Bank in Paris or a trattoria near the Piazza Navona in Rome. You enter the restaurant. What's the first thing that catches your eye?

1. The paintings on the wall?
2. The antipasto table?
3. The dessert tray?

If you answered number one, you should concentrate on the Louvre and the Sistine Chapel. You should certainly read no further into "The Pastry Principle," because one of the world's great ideas will fail to excite you.

If you answered number two, the idea is intriguing but not urgent. If you answered number three, this chapter will improve your life.

I am, obviously, passionate about desserts. When I enter a restaurant I hover around the dessert selection, already beginning to consider my choice. When I read a menu my eye travels like a locomotive, nonstop, straight to the confections at the bottom. Through Potage St. Germain and Veal Cordon Bleu my mind never ceases to consider which combination of desserts is closest to heaven.

Combination? Of course! A dessert lover can hardly settle for a single napoleon, for a single scoop of chocolate mousse, while leaving the other desserts untried. A dessert lover always wants at least two desserts.

Of course he or she does not necessarily want to *pay* for two desserts; he wants the second dessert free. This is not accomplished without a plan.

It is only fair to point out that in many of the two- and three-star restaurants in France they *assume* you want to try all the desserts. They will be listed on the menu as *Le Chariot des Desserts* or *La Farandole des Desserts*, and in effect you are ordering the dessert tray. Taste whatever you wish.

It is also true that in many of the $40-a-head restaurants of Paris you can ask for a second dessert and get it free, if that's your definition of *free*.

The Pastry Principle is essential when you're eating cheap, at $20-a-head and under. If $20-a-head surprises you, you haven't been to Paris recently. The principle is remarkably simple and requires nothing more than an adventurous spirit and a healthy appetite.

The principle states: In order to get two desserts for the price of one, you simply tell the waiter that you would like to try two desserts—a half portion of each. In almost any language you can manage, "Half of this and half of that."

Surely there's nothing wrong with that. Nothing deceitful, nothing crass, no sleight of hand. You're not asking for anything extra, just a different arrangement. In my twenty years of traveling no restaurant has ever denied such an innocent request.

Now, here's what happens. It is *impossible* for a restaurant to serve only half a dessert. Oh yes, I suppose it *could* be done. I suppose a waiter could attempt to cut that cherry tart so thin that it would be no more than a sliver. But it never happens. The waiter knows that if he tries to cut a cherry tart thin he ends up with a lot of loose cherries and a messy-looking dessert. So the *least* he gives you is three-quarters of a piece. To this you add a "half" portion of what appears to be a Parisian version of lemon meringue pie, and you're on your way.

I don't suppose I have to explain why you order a half portion of lemon meringue pie. If you don't know that much, you'll never master this system. I can only suggest that you *try* to cut anything less than a full portion of lemon meringue pie. Impossible.

This brings us to variations on the theme, and I do think you need a certain working understanding of desserts. You could, if you married a tablespoon of chocolate mousse to a paper-thin French apple torte, end up with only one dessert. The Pastry Principle demands that you consider which desserts cannot be served in less than a full portion. Most of them cannot. A towering chocolate cake really cannot. Lemon meringue, obviously not. Nor can any pie or tart with a fruit filling, because the filling will not stay inside the pie and the waiter ends up serving a pudding.

Better yet are cream and custard inventions. Some restaurants specialize in the napoleon, which usually rests temptingly on the dessert tray in the form of a long rectangle. It takes a waiter four years in the best pastry kitchens of Paris and Brussels just to learn how to cut a *full* piece. Even a three-quarter piece ends in disaster.

What about puddings, sherbets, and mousses? Perhaps you think they are the exception to the rule. Perhaps you think that it takes only a tablespoon to serve a Cassis Sorbet, a lemon mousse, or a Zuppa Inglese. Technically you are not wrong, but it would also require a waiter without a conscience. Even if he *wanted* to serve a half portion of lemon mousse, he would see how lonely it looked even with a half portion of Zuppa Inglese beside it. No, he figures, these are nice people and I've been working hard through the whole dinner. No sense ruining it now.

Cakes? Well, it's true that a low-level Sachertorte can be managed, but never worry about those seven-story coconut creations. They can't be cut thin without toppling, and the waiter is too proud of his dessert tray to topple them. Result: a full portion.

Then there are desserts like Floating Island, a caramel-coated meringue resting in an egg custard bath. A triumph of visual artistry. No waiter or captain would dare serve a half portion—it would look so inelegant. No, nothing less than *all* will do.

Finally, there is one more variation on the system. It insures your getting at least two desserts, maybe two-and-a-half. Again it calls for an elementary understanding of the science of pastries and puddings.

They wheel over the dessert tray. You notice that there's only one large piece left of lemon meringue pie, or only one large portion of Crème Caramel. The lemon meringue is already nervously bobbing and weaving. Cut it in half? Of course not. Even if the waiter wanted to try, what would he do with the other half? He'd have to prop it up. So you own the lemon meringue, and in fact the waiter is delighted to serve it to you, thus preventing it from toppling over into the chocolate mousse.

The same rule would hold for the Crème Caramel. The waiter can't leave himself with a half portion. He can't serve it, and besides, it looks lonely on the dessert tray. You get it all.

Easy? It's absolutely simple. And don't for a moment think you are offending the waiter or captain. Dessert is one course where a captain can show special attention. After all, what can he do with a potage or a Coq au Vin? The restaurant doesn't "count" desserts; the captain serves what he wishes. And it *is* getting awfully close to check time. Which is not to suggest that the captain or waiter is mercenary. On the contrary; they want you to enjoy the restaurant and to appreciate the service. An extra dessert hardly matters.

Of course, to me it matters a lot, and for twenty years I've been using the Pastry Principle. It has never failed, and only once has it been embarrassing. That wasn't even in Europe, but right at home in New York City. I met my match at The Four Seasons over a piece of chocolate fudge cake.

It was dessert time at The Four Seasons and I had been contemplating the tray for about two hours. As it rolled by, back and forth, my eyes followed it like a tennis match. As the last piece of a particularly endearing creation was snatched away by someone at another table, I held my breath until the kitchen sent out a replacement. And all along I kept my eye on a chocolate fudge cake that appeared to be getting considerable attention from the regulars.

There was one large piece of the fudge cake remaining on the tray when it came my turn to order dessert. Time for the Pastry Principle.

"I'll have a half portion of the fudge cake and a half portion of the Nesselrode pie," I said, aware that I would end up with a full portion of each.

The captain considered my request with appropriate reserve. "The chocolate fudge cake is very heavy," he said. "Why don't you have the fudge cake first and let me hold your portion of Nesselrode pie? If you can still handle it, it will be there."

Still handle it? Fighting words, I thought.

"O.K.," I answered with some arrogance, "but don't go far with that Nesselrode pie. I can handle it."

The captain bowed once or twice and I charged into the fudge cake. Let me tell you about the chocolate fudge cake at The Four Seasons—it's solid fudge. And not only that, it is to fudge what lead is to metal. I ate three forkfuls. Incredibly delicious, but my digestive system was rebelling.

The captain danced by with the dessert tray, pointing to the Nesselrode pie to confirm that he was holding it for me.

I took two more bites. I begged Rita to take a bite. I had hardly finished half of it. The captain walked by again. I could tell by his suggestion of a smile that he knew I was done in.

I smiled right back and took a particularly large bite so he could see how well I was doing, but it was a last gasp effort. Even the thought of the Nesselrode pie was unbearable.

I surrendered meekly, humiliated, and gave the captain an outrageously large tip to compensate for my embarrassment.

I pass along this story so that future Pastry Principle users may profit from my error. You must understand that all great ideas have their excesses and all great innovators suffer defeats. So it was at The Four Seasons. It was not that the principle didn't work, but that it worked too well.

Never Bring a Camera

Ninety-nine out of a hundred travelers bring a camera, and I've been one of the ninety-nine. I have photographs of every cathedral in Italy. I have my wife in front of every national monument in Madrid. I have our guides, our cars, the flea markets, the cute café on the Left Bank. I can bore you for three and a half hours and sixteen cities. And I have finally concluded it is a mistake to bring a camera to Europe.

I know I'm flying in the face of convention, but I'm serious about this, and I've thought about it for a long time. I don't think any of us quite realize what we lose when we bring a camera with us. I first realized what I was losing when I dragged some friends through my slide collection of Italian cathedrals.

"Hey, everyone, how would you like to see the slides of our trip to Italy?"

Silence.

"Oh, you'll love them, and it will take only a few minutes. I'll go get them."

Seventeen churches follow, with painfully familiar dialogue. But at the eighteenth church . . .

"And here's Rita in front of the Church of St. Francis in Assisi." (As though someone were having trouble figuring out it was Rita.) "Notice that I didn't get the exact light reading."

"What's inside the church?" someone yawned.

"Inside the church?" My goodness, *I never went inside the church.*

I remember the day. The sun smiled for a brief half hour. I leaped into the backseat of our rented car for the camera. I hadn't missed a church picture yet. I gauged the sun, set the distance. No good—bad angle.

"Rita, would you run around to the other side so I can get the columns? Please hurry—the sun's going down."

Sound familiar?

Anyway, I got the church, and we climbed back into the car. And we never went inside.

All we missed was the greatest collection of Giotto frescoes in the whole wide world. Maybe one of the ten most important works of the entire Italian Renaissance.

I realized, as I continued to show the slides, that I had not *seen* what I had photographed. I had a good idea of the facades, and if I saw the churches in travel brochures I would recognize them. But I had no sense of their spirit, of their meaning. My eye saw only through the lens of the camera.

The more I thought about it, the more true it became. I was a camera slave. As we would drive through a town in Italy, I searched it for snapshots. My eye looked for angles, for shadows, for depth and background. The camera's eye became my eye and I saw what I hoped the camera would see.

It's not as obvious as that. I didn't drive into town, stop the car, and take a light reading. It was more subtle, sort of semiconscious, and therefore more insidious. You never really know how much pull the camera has.

I know that a lot of Italy passed me by. I have great photos, but my mental image of the country exists in two-by-three-inch rectangles. If I lose my photo album, I won't remember a thing.

And, of course, in my frenzy to have everything on 120 Kodak Color, I sometimes failed to visit inside. Having preserved the image, I must have sensed a feeling of completion.

You will say that the camera is only an adjunct. That *you* see all there is to see, and then photograph the highlights. I don't think so. A camera has a life of its own. When it hangs around your neck it demands a certain consciousness. It has you looking for the sun. It has you thinking F-5.6. You never own a camera—it owns you.

You will say that you can see a city and still think about taking snapshots. Well, you can, but it's celluloid thinking. It's a compromise. While you are deeply involved in the stunning experience of Michelangelo's *David*, there is that little man inside the camera tugging on your sleeve.

The following summer I went to France without a camera. I discovered immediately that I could buy better pictures than I had

taken. But mainly, I felt a sense of freedom as though a knapsack had been taken off my back.

In Italy, I had always felt that there was a fence between me and the country. That I stood on one side and looked across. That I was recording a country instead of living in it. It's easy to feel that way. You take photographs and you think you possess the country. Not at all—you possess the photographs.

In France, without a camera to photograph the other side of the fence, I walked across. I talked to everyone and wandered everywhere. I played tennis in Beaune and Cannes, and basketball in St. Tropez. In Italy I would have taken pictures of the basketball game, and that would have been it. In France I marched right in and asked to play. What a difference! After the game I had five friends, each eager to recommend his favorite restaurant.

I urge you to try it. You will enjoy a different experience and have a new sense of where you have been. I know it's a radical suggestion. Bringing a camera is something we take for granted. It's a habit—we wouldn't think of traveling without it.

Give it some thought. Some habits deserve to be broken.

Your Friends Took 300 Slides of London— Do You Really Want to See Them?

If you're going to leave your camera home, and not show everyone your slides of Europe, you certainly should be spared seeing theirs. We all know that the reason we sit through our friends' slide programs is that we expect them to sit through ours. But let's be honest about this: Is there anything worse than spending an evening at a friend's home looking at slides of his trip to Europe?

I say there's nothing worse. Those of you who disagree can have my current, up-to-date list of friends who have just returned. They will be glad to hear from you and to show you their photos. You think you're imposing? Not at all! People who take snapshots delight in showing them to *anyone*. Garbage men have been interrupted from their routes. Delivery boys have been corralled. Plumbers and electricians are particularly vulnerable. People with photos of their trip are absolute maniacs about showing them.

I'm not a maniac about seeing them, however. My body seems to contract all sorts of illnesses as soon as friends return from Europe. My wife doesn't seem to feel that scarlet fever is sufficient reason for declining an invitation, so I rise from my deathbed to spend a few unbearable hours looking at monuments and cathedrals. Doesn't anyone take photographs of anything else?

Usually there are four or five couples called together on a Saturday evening for this ritual. I always hope that nobody will ask to see the photos, but that has never happened. Somehow the photos have some strange sense of inevitability about them. From the moment I walk in the door I know it's only minutes until the question is raised.

"Mona, we're all dying to see your photographs of London. Will we get a chance to see them?"

"Oh, really, they're nothing." (A word of truth!) "I don't think you'd be interested. Just Ronnie and I visiting a few spots."

There should be silence at this point. After all, someone has asked and has been told "no," so that should be the end of it, right? Wrong! Some other guest will always tally a few points on the social scorecard by saying, "We'd love to." (Maybe *she* would.)

"Well then," says the hostess, "perhaps just a few. Ronnie, why don't you bring up the carton from the basement? Take Arthur with you to help."

And thus begins the dialogue:

"Here's a shot of Ronnie waving at me from the steps of the House of Commons."

Yep, that's Ronnie all right, and that's what he's doing, waving. Terrific.

Thereafter unfolds a series of photos of Ronnie waving in front of eighty-seven buildings in a row. It takes three hours. I can't stand it.

Once I thought I had a solution. It occurred to me that most people must feel the same way I do and that the only thing missing was a little candor. The hostess might really care about whether her guests wanted to see France's 1,216 cathedrals. It happened like this:

"Mona, we're absolutely breathless to see your photos of France."

"Oh, come on. They're so dull. Nobody really wants . . ."

"Yes, Mona, we all do."

"Well, I'm going to show them only if everybody wants to see them, and I want everybody to be absolutely honest."

At this point, some guy (not me) says, "Well, to tell the truth . . ."

But Mona is too quick for him. "All right then, if you all absolutely insist."

Sensing my moment, I chip in with, "I think John sort of suggested that he would rather not, and actually, I would rather not—that is, since you're asking us all to be absolutely honest."

"Well, why don't *you* read a magazine then while everyone else looks at the slides? And why don't you let John speak for himself!"

"Oh, I'd love to see them," says John, whose wife is standing by his side jabbing her nail file into his back. And I hate to tell you about the look *my* wife is flashing across the room.

So, if you ever learned that honesty is the best policy, forget it. It's usually the worst policy.

After that evening I gave a lot of thought to the problem. There had to be some way to solve it. Robert Benchley once wrote about a way to deal with people who talk endlessly about their trips. He always asked them if they had visited a particular town along the route. They hadn't. Of course not—there was no such town. Having untracked the dialogue, Benchley went on to say that he couldn't believe they had missed this town, and how it was the high point of his trip. In about five minutes he put the whole thing to bed.

That's what Benchley did. No wonder everyone said he was a genius.

The thing is, you can't *not be interested*. You can't yawn. You can't look at your watch. You can't be honest about it. And scarlet fever is not enough of an excuse to miss it. What then is to be done?

Only one thing. You have to be *extremely* interested. You must be beside yourself with delight, feverish with curiosity.

And so the next time we were at Mona's (maybe Gloria's) I was really interested.

"Here's Ronnie waving at us from in front of Charles Dickens's house outside of London . . ."

"Charles Dickens's house? Really? That's very interesting. It's still standing? I think that's awfully interesting. How many rooms are there in the house?"

"I'm not sure about the rooms . . ."

"Well, when did he live there?"

"I think it was in his early years."

"Before or after he wrote *David Copperfield*?"

"I'm not sure about that . . ."

"Let's look it up. Where's the encyclopedia?"

Mona is getting a little anxious. "Maybe we ought to go on to the second slide . . ."

"No, no—we can't. Not until we at least find out when he lived there. Maybe he wrote *Nicholas Nickleby* there or something. That's one hell of a slide!"

At this point you run to get the encyclopedia and immediately start reading about the life of Charles Dickens. It's best if they have the *Encyclopaedia Britannica*. After five minutes of the *Britannica* any slide program is in serious jeopardy.

"Leonard, we all appreciate your interest in the slide, but we must get on. Here's our second slide of Ronnie, standing in front of the house of William Shakespeare."

"William Shakespeare! Stratford-on-Avon? This is exciting! What's the address?"

"Address? There's no address. They didn't have addresses in those days."

"You're right. That's a good point. Who did he live with?"

"I don't know. His sister, maybe." (Mona's voice is getting a little edgy.)

"I don't think Shakespeare *had* a sister. Let's look it up."

"Leonard, I don't think anyone *cares* who he lived there with."

"I care," pipes up John. Remember John? The coward? (I love him.)

By this time you have the encyclopedia and are enthusiastically reading about Shakespeare and the Dark Lady of the sonnets, and you can hardly control yourself.

"I think he lived there with the Dark Lady!" you shout.

"The Dark Lady!" chimes in John. "Hey, that guy Shakespeare was all right. What else does it say about him, Len?"

So you read another five minutes from the *Britannica,* and we're still on slide number two.

At this point everyone is getting fidgety. The encyclopedia is giving them a big pain. Shakespeare is giving them a big pain. And the whole slide operation isn't faring any better. The hostess spots this, and I see her put about 300 slides back into the carton. I guess she figures that if we're going to have a twenty-minute discussion about each slide, she can fit in only three slides an hour.

"Only eight more slides," she says gaily, and flashes on number three.

"Here's me standing in front of Samuel Johnson's house in London."

Silence.

"This is one of London's most interesting sights," she says.

"Very interesting," I say.

"*Very* interesting," John says.

Mona doesn't know what to do. She's committed to only eight slides and she can see her whole vacation flashing before her eyes in only twenty minutes. She really can't move on to slide number four. But the room is silent and a few people are clearing their throats. One of them is me. You have to clear your throat a lot with scarlet fever.

Finally Mona turns to slide number four. It's Ronnie again, standing in front of something. Nobody asks what.

Mona springs forward into action, but her rhythm has been broken and she can't seem to get it on track again. She says a few things and we move right along to slide number eight.

"A very interesting group of slides," I say, standing up and stretching.

And the program is over.

There are a few courteous remarks about how lovely their trip must have been and how they captured the essence of London in the slides, and then the conversation turns to the urgent matters of the day like Off-Track Betting.

A few bourbons on-the-rocks quickly bury that uneasy feeling that everyone has about the slides, and everyone is soon having a great time. Even the hostess senses the spirit in the room and doesn't feel too badly about the photos.

And that is the way to sabotage a Three-Hour Slide Program.

At least, that *was* the way. Now that it's been revealed, it may not be effective any longer. But by the same reasoning, the Monas of America have also been informed, and perhaps they will consider some editing. They had better. Because where oppression is great, the people will always find a way to rise up against it.

Bring Your Tennis Racket

O.K., enough of language courses and camera settings. Let's get to the important stuff—tennis. Almost everybody traveling to Europe leaves his tennis racket home. I think that's a mistake.

It is understandable though. You don't think of Copenhagen or Madrid as places to play tennis. You think more in terms of guided tours, museums, and unusual restaurants. Besides, you don't know where the courts are, you don't have anyone to play with, and you don't speak the language. These sound like obstacles, but they're not. The courts are all over the city, someone will be glad to arrange a game for you, and all the language you need to know to play tennis is about eight words.

There are some other arguments that favor bringing your racket. First, your regular tennis partner, Norman, is spending his two-week vacation at a tennis resort, getting lessons from Arthur Ashe. Give him two weeks to get his backhand straightened out and he'll smash you off the court. Second, how are you going to handle the ten pounds that you'll gain on Coq au Vin or Veal Pizzaiola? You think riding the elevators at the Eiffel Tower takes off much weight?

So you have to agree that it's not a bad idea, after a day in the Louvre or the Prado, to head for the tennis courts at 3:30 in the afternoon.

I may sound knowledgeable about this, but the first time I packed my racket and wristbands I really had no great expectations. It was just that I had looked at our itinerary and prayed that somewhere hidden among the castles and cathedrals there must be a tennis court. Certainly it would be asphalt, and there would be grass growing in between the cracks. Certainly there would be no fence, or if there was a fence it would be too close to the back lines. Certainly there would be no players. I think this approximates the thinking of the average American traveler. Doesn't anyone stop to think about how Spain fields a Davis Cup team?

Admittedly I didn't, but I hoped and prayed, and I'm now prepared to tell you—tennis nuts of America—that you can play all the tennis you want in France; there are courts in every city. Not only that, there are tennis courts in every city in Portugal. I'll bet you didn't even know they play tennis in Portugal.

The first time I ever played tennis in Europe was in the town of Beaune, France, the center of the Burgundy wine district. As we drove up to our hotel I noticed tennis courts only a block away.

"I'm going to play tennis," I told Rita.

"You'll be back in fifteen minutes," she said.

Now it is true that I could handle some French—a point that a number of maître d's didn't fully agree with—but even if I couldn't, I could have managed the situation with little difficulty. Most Europeans speak a little English, certainly in the large cities, and even in the smaller cities like Beaune. And after all, how much language is needed? You walk into the club in tennis whites carrying your racket. You're obviously American. (They know. They know.) A guy walks up to you, points to his racket, points to an empty court, and you're playing.

All you need is some courage. You have to walk onto a court or into a club in a foreign city and ask for a game. Surprise. You will find the members anxious to help you out. There is sort of a fraternity of tennis players throughout the world, and when a New Yorker steps into a tennis club in Beaune they are extremely cordial.

Don't be dissuaded by a *private* club. Walk right in and politely ask to play. Even people at a private club realize that you are a guest in their country, and they will treat you like one. I've never been treated any other way.

So you can count on getting a game, and you can count on someone nearby speaking enough English to help you—if you need help, which is not likely.

I played two sets of doubles that first day, and tennis was only half the fun. After the match I had three friends. While we cooled off, they talked to me about the city, pointing out places that were not in the tourist guides, suggesting restaurants, telling me about themselves—and insisting that we play again tomorrow.

I'll tell you how lucky you can be. As we sat and talked, one of the young men pointed to a gentleman playing singles on the next court. He was Monsieur du Villaine, the proprietor of the Domaine of Romanée Conti, the most distinguished vineyard in all of Burgundy and perhaps in all the world. Would I like to meet him? And who do you think got invited to visit the cellars of Romanée Conti the next day—which might be like a French tourist in New York getting invited to dinner with David Rockefeller?

I floated back to the hotel, tore up our list of recommended restaurants, and told Rita we were dining at Mère Michel's and that dinner had already been called in for us. And I casually dropped the name of the greatest vineyard in Burgundy, where we were invited for a private visit to the cellars.

I played all through France, and the next summer I played up and down the coastal cities of Portugal. Portugal is a poor country, and there are always three or four nine-year-old ball boys servicing every court. After the match you tip them fifteen escudos (about 28¢) between them. It's not much of a tip, but then again you can buy a helluva lunch in Portugal for fifty escudos.

Watch out, if you've never played with ball boys before. It's a much faster game. You never get that restful stroll to the net. With four ball boys you have a ball in your hand every second. It's always in play. I was tired at 2–1 in the first set until I got used to it.

I ran into some unexpected local customs on the courts in Portugal. For one thing, nobody keeps score. I think it's considered poor taste to keep score—like maybe you're too interested in winning. I'm not sure, but I was playing a doubles match in Viana do Castelo, at the northern end of Portugal, and the score was 2–1. At this point everyone walks to the net and asks the score, and nobody knows it. I know it, of course, but I figure that if nobody else knows it after seven minutes of playing, maybe I shouldn't know it either. Everybody is courteous, and we finally get it settled and return to serious business. We play two more games and the score is now 3–2, and—you may not believe this—everybody walks to the net again and asks the score.

Another curious thing happened in Portugal. I was playing this real-good-guy and I was playing over my head and beating him 5–3. It's my serve and I'm really concentrating, and as I get ready for the first toss he waves his arms. I assume he got something in his eye or he pulled a muscle, but anyway we both walk to the net.

He says, "Let's try my balls. I think they're a little more lively."

I'm fuming, but I take his balls, and proceed to smash my first serve somewhere near the locker room. In short, I double-fault three times and lose the game. I also lose the next game, and it's 5-5.

At this point I settle down. My international reputation is at stake and my confidence returns. It's my serve, and my first serve goes in four times in a row. Unbelievable! He has no trouble with it (nobody has ever failed to return my serve in fifteen years of playing tennis), but my forehand returns are devastating. The score is 6-5 mine. I'm brimming with confidence; he looks worried.

Suddenly he waves his arms again and motions to the ball boys. About six ball boys rush onto the court and start to brush down the clay. Not only that, but they hose it. I'm going out of my mind; he's smiling gently. Twenty minutes later we get back on the court and he runs out three straight games for 8-6. I'm still wondering whether my friend was extraordinarily polite or a terrific hustler.

Either way, let me say this: The Portuguese are delightful. They welcomed me in their clubs and simply couldn't do enough for me. I think I like tennis better in Portugal than in New York.

Maybe you think I'm a top-notch player and can get on the court with anyone and hold my own. And maybe you're just an average player and worried about looking foolish if you ask for a game on a foreign court. Don't worry. First of all, I'm an average player with an unreliable backhand and a second serve that hardly makes it over the net. Learn to say, "I'm an average player," or "I'm a good player," and they will pair you properly.

I played tennis every day in Portugal, and again, my tennis friends drove me around town and told me where to buy the best bottles of port, and where to have lunch for fifty escudos.

It is an absolutely marvelous way to visit a country. You can still see the cathedrals, but not all of them. You can get exercise, and you can get to know a country in a way that you never expected.

And, if you're playing at home with a guy named Norman, he'll probably think you're spending your whole vacation in the cathedrals, and relax his game. When you get back, you'll destroy him.

How to Make a Million Dollars on Your Vacation

Hardly anybody goes on vacation now without hoping for rain. The reason is a thing called rain insurance. If you buy it, and it rains all the time you're on vacation, the insurance company pays you a lot of money.

But if you buy rain insurance and the weather is all sunny and nice, and you have a terrific time, you lose. You don't collect any money on your insurance.

So it's no wonder that everybody is searching for new places to go on vacation. Puerto Rico is in plenty of trouble and St. Thomas is desperate. But Miami Beach isn't complaining. Everyone says it rains there all the time.

Everything is getting all mixed up. And the fault lies with the insurance companies, which offer:

3 OUT OF EVERY 4 VACATION DAYS RAIN-FREE
OR YOU COLLECT UP TO $100 A DAY

Not only that, but there's a big picture in the brochure of a couple laughing and having a great time—and it's raining like hell. At $100 a day, who could blame them?

So it was, when Rita asked where I wanted to go on a recent vacation, I had no trouble answering:

"Mobile, Alabama."

"Mobile, Alabama? What's in Mobile, Alabama?"

"Terrific grilled cheese sandwiches."

"Come on, no fooling around, what do they have there? Some new palatial hotel?"

"Well, I wouldn't say that, but it's called The Garden Spot of Southern Alabama."

"Well, what do they have to see?"

"A very important statue of Jefferson Davis."

"You're just kidding me! I'm going to look it up—it probably has the best weather in the Southeast."

"You're getting close," I assured her. "It has the worst weather in the Southeast, and probably in the whole country."

"The worst weather?" she questioned.

"The most rain in the country!"

"Well, what are we going to do there?"

"They have an outstanding public library."

"I'm not going!" she said.

"I don't think you understand," I said. "There's no percentage going to a place where it's sunny. It costs you a lot of money and all you get out of it is a good time. Don't you know about rain insurance?"

"I think I do—you buy insurance against rain, and if it rains a lot on your vacation you get some of your money back."

"That's right," I said.

"So what about it?"

"Well, let's say you buy rain insurance, and it costs you $40 for a ten-day policy. If it rains all ten days you get back $700. So what are you going to hope for?"

"You're absolutely right!" she said.

"Shall I book us to Mobile?"

"Wait a minute," she said. "I heard Olga in the beauty parlor say that she just came back from Dallas and the weather was terrible."

"Not bad, but it rains more in Mobile."

"What about the rain forest in Puerto Rico? It never *stops* raining there."

"A great idea," I assured her, "but the insurance company thought of it first. Rain forests are excluded from the policy."

"Bunch of hustlers," she said.

"How about a ski vacation? It always rains when we go skiing."

"Ski vacations are excluded," I said.

"Terrific policy; they sell you rain insurance, and then they make you go on vacation where it's sunny."

"It's a rotten deal," I agreed.

"Well, why did you pick Mobile?"

"I wrote away to the U.S. Weather Bureau in Silver Springs, Maryland, and I got the latest list of all the main cities and how much rain they get. Mobile gets the most."

"Does *any* place beat it?"

"Yakutat, Alaska, beats it."

"Let's go there," she said.

"It's too expensive. We'd waste all our money on plane fare and not make enough profit on the insurance."

"Now, you say Mobile gets the *most* rain, but does it get the most *days* of rain? Maybe Mobile gets all of its rain on one day."

"If it does, the whole southern half of Alabama gets washed out into the Gulf Stream."

"What's bad about that?" she said.

Her question was fair, so I rushed to the Weather Bureau chart. Sure enough, Mobile gets the *most* rain, but not the most days of rain. Olympia, Washington, gets the most days of rain, but for that kind of plane fare you could go to Yakutat. Short of the Pacific Northwest, Youngstown, Ohio, leads the list.

"We're not going to Mobile," I said. "We're going to Youngstown, Ohio."

"Thanks," she said. "How about a second choice?"

"Second choice is Beckley, West Virginia."

"I'll take Youngstown."

But Rita brightened up as soon as she started to count all the money we were going to make, and we booked our flight to Youngstown.

The flight was uneventful except for a lightning-and-thunderstorm that got Rita very excited. Usually I have trouble getting her on a flight when it's sunny. Nothing will ever be the same.

"Do we collect if it rains on the flight?" she asked.

"I don't know," I said. "But anyway, who knows if it's raining on the ground? If it rains on the *ground*, I think we collect."

"Could you ask the pilot to fly very low so we can find out?" she asked.

We arrived that evening and checked into the hotel. We called the weather report right away. "Rain for tomorrow," they said.

"Great!"

I brought my tennis racket just in case I could sneak in a few sets between downpours. The next morning Rita woke me at nine.

"Put on your tennis shorts," she said.

"My tennis shorts? Why? Isn't it raining out?"

"It's beautiful."

So we had breakfast and I trudged over to the tennis courts and arranged a foursome. What a day—not a cloud in the sky. Looked like a washout (a sun-out) for our insurance.

At around 11:30 the sky darkened suddenly and we all raced for the clubhouse.

"Looks like it'll really come down," I said gleefully.

Everyone looked at me.

Fact is, it didn't rain at all, and everyone dashed back onto the courts. I was so mad that I double-faulted three times in a row and hit one backhand into the swimming pool.

We still had the afternoon left and we were praying desperately for rain, but the skies were clear. It was wrecking our vacation.

We were getting pretty tense about it. At about 2:30 Rita was sunning herself in a lounge chair by the side of the pool, and she suddenly shouted:

"It's raining! It's raining!"

"It's not raining at all!" I screamed. "You got splashed."

And it didn't rain at all the whole day.

The next day we had breakfast at 8:30 and toured Youngstown's cultural centers and important monuments. We were back at a quarter to ten. I was too depressed to play tennis, so we went to see a revival of *Butch Cassidy and the Sundance Kid.*

We dashed outside when they started to play "Raindrops Keep Falling on My Head." But there wasn't a cloud in sight.

The following day we went to see *Butch Cassidy* again.

Three days, and it hadn't rained. Fifteen years we've been going away on vacations, and we've *never* had three sunny days in a row.

The next day we toured Youngstown again. Look, I don't want to be unkind to Youngstown. It has enough troubles already with 169 days of rain or snow a year. That means there are only 196 days without rain or snow.

It has a fine university and library, but it's a steel mill town, and I don't even think the town fathers would make a strong argument for a vacation there.

As for the 169 days of precipitation, Youngstown didn't use up any of them during the ten days that we were there.

We packed our bags and flew home and couldn't collect a cent on our insurance.

Let me make it clear that our unfortunate experience should not discourage other vacationers from seeking out rainy spots. There's a buck to make here and every red-blooded American ought to take a shot at it. There are a lot of possibilities I hadn't considered.

For instance, we didn't check which month it rains most in Youngstown. Maybe Youngstown has a rainy season. Maybe some other city has a rainy season. Maybe you can catch Mobile when those Gulf storms are tearing in.

And then there's the whole rest of the world. I mean, if you don't mind going to Guam, it rained 272 days there during 1978. Who knows what it does in Tibet or the Congo?

The way to do it is to find a place like Guam and take your whole family there. Better than that, take your family and everybody else's family along and cover them all for the maximum. Stay away for a month and if it rains 75% of the time (which it does on Guam) you collect about a million dollars. For that kind of money, you can have a terrific vacation anywhere.

The Emergency Restaurant Guide

Now that you've made a million on rain insurance, you're ready for the best of everything—the most luxurious hotels, the classiest jewelry shops, and the finest restaurants. Certainly the finest restaurants. That raises a problem: Great restaurants are hard to find.

You might say, "Why don't you just check them out in the guidebooks?" But I've tried that and I'm not satisfied. So I was discussing the problem with my friend Sheldon, the gourmet, and Sheldon has a few ideas for scouting the best restaurants in any city on a moment's notice.

I don't want to exaggerate Sheldon's concern about food, but his wife says that the only way she could get him to the Louvre was to tell him that they specialize in Sole Veronique. Maybe that's true and maybe it's not, but there's no question that Sheldon is a world-class eater in Paris, Rome, or at Dubrow's Cafeteria in New York.

Now, a world-class eater is not likely to be satisfied choosing his restaurants from the guidebooks, and this was Sheldon's problem—how to choose the *really* great restaurants in any city at any time. After years of research he has discovered the answer, which he graciously passed on to me over a double cheeseburger with everything, at McDonald's.

"The problem is," says Sheldon, "that the guidebooks and the travel writers do a decent job, but they're writing for the average traveler, not for the eater. You won't be disappointed if you follow them, but you won't be ecstatic. Furthermore, a travel writer visits a city once a year and tries the restaurants once a year. Another year goes by before his opinion gets into print. I can't go by that."

"It's a tough problem," I agreed.

"You know," he said, "in New York there are forty-five writers studying the restaurants. A chef can't even have an argument with a maître d' without it getting reported in four newspapers and two magazines. In Rome a chef could retire, the restaurant could go straight downhill, and you wouldn't find out about it for two years."

"You have a system, Sheldon, for dealing with this problem?"

"Yes, I do, and it's sensational. It has worked flawlessly for five years. It's simple, cheap, and absolutely reliable."

I got out my pad to copy down the system. I figured it would be full of code symbols, stars, crossed knives and forks, and lots of secret stuff. Sheldon waved his arm. "Put the pad away," he said. No doubt he wanted to avoid any written record, names of royalty, unlisted phone numbers.

"O.K.," he said, "we know who doesn't have the latest word about the restaurants. The travel writers don't. The guidebooks don't. The tourist offices certainly don't. And the concierges in the hotels only send you to restaurants where their uncle is a partner."

"All right, Sheldon, I understand the problem. What's the answer?"

"Well, in every city there are the gourmets—the people who dine out constantly, who entertain, who *know* the best restaurants."

"They're listed in the Yellow Pages?"

"Don't be wise, Leonard. I'm about to reveal the system of the century and you're being wise. It'll still be a system even if I don't tell you about it."

"O.K., I'm sorry, Sheldon. You were saying there are these sophisticates . . ."

"Right. Now where would you find them?"

"Sitting in the park?"

"Very hilarious."

"No kidding, Sheldon, I give up. Where do you find them?"

"Well, in every city there are certain elegant stores. Jewelry shops, furs, or perhaps an art gallery. Not the tourist shops where you go to buy some trinkets for the folks back home. The real stuff. The Tiffany, Cartier, Van Cleef & Arpels."

"I just walk in and ask the owner about restaurants?"

"Of course not, but the chances are that your wife will want to visit the shop anyway, so you walk in and start to look at the jewelry."

"I thought you said this system wasn't expensive."

"You don't buy anything, you just look. After about three minutes you stop looking and start gazing around the store with sort of a bored expression. You'll be bored anyway, so it's easy. But while you're at it you start looking for the owner."

"He has a sign on him that says 'owner'?"

"I don't know why I'm telling you this, Leonard, you'll never pull it off. But the fact is that it's always easy to spot the owner. He'll look like the British ambassador and he'll be circulating around the shop keeping an eye on everything. I promise you, you can't miss him. After you spot him you kind of stroll over to where he is standing, clasp your hands behind your back, and look up at the chandelier. You present the picture of the bored husband whose wife has dragged him to the shop, and you're trying to make the best of it. You also present the picture of a guy who has a few bucks hanging around just in case his wife happens to find a gold bracelet that she can't live without. The proprietor is bound to turn to you and say, 'Can I help you?'

" 'Well, my wife is looking around,' you say.

"The proprietor understands. Half the husbands in the store have been dragged there. He'll try to engage you in conversation just so that you don't lose patience altogether and walk out—with the money, that is.

" 'First visit to Copenhagen?' he'll ask.

" 'Yes, it is. Second day, in fact.'

" 'Finding it interesting?'

" 'Oh yes, very.'

" 'Enjoying anything in particular?'

" 'Well, what we'd really like are a few excellent restaurants.'

"At this, the proprietor looks you over carefully. He knows every restaurant in the city. He knows every menu in the city. The question is, where to send you. But the mere fact that you are shopping in his store and that your wife is looking at $500 bracelets establishes some credentials. Nevertheless you must say to him, 'We're just interested in good food. We don't care whether Mama cooks it in the back kitchen or three maître d's cook it at the table. We don't care whether they speak English or not. I think we would like the kind of restaurant that you and your family would go to if you wanted a fine dinner in Copenhagen.'

"His eyes will twinkle. He's being asked about a matter on which he is an expert. Experts always delight in talking about their expertise.

" 'First of all, there is Belle Terrasse—still the best restaurant in Copenhagen. But remember to go before seven or after nine. It's too crowded in between and the service gets sloppy. Start off with Fond d'Artichaut Perouges. That's warm artichoke bottoms, pâté de foie gras, and mushrooms in cream, glazed with Gruyère cheese and a blessing from heaven. After that, the Darne de Saumon Cuicinière. Elegant. And do be sure to try our aquavit. You can get martinis in New York.

" 'Next try Krogs Fiskerestaurant. Ask for Hans, and here, give him my card. He'll take care of you. They have a specialty called The Fish. When a fish restaurant describes one of its specialties as *The* Fish, you can't go far wrong. It is, in fact, a fillet of sole steamed in Rhine wine with tarragon leaves. Sound good?

" 'Now write this down. Here's a restaurant that's a bit out of the way and doesn't even have an English menu. The waiters speak English, however, and you're safe in their hands. The name is Bjornekaelderen—that's why I wanted you to write it down. Not many tourists get there. Perhaps because they're afraid to pronounce it. I think it is one of the best in the city.'

"And so on. In five minutes you will have ten restaurants and you will have them from the best source in Copenhagen. At this point you hope that your wife has chosen something for $15 and not $500. You thank the owner kindly, and take off for Bjornekaelderen."

Sheldon smiled broadly. "The system has never failed," he said.

And so it is that my friend Sheldon, of humble origin but with seven gold medals for eating, has solved one of the culinary problems of all time. Nothing flashy, nothing sophisticated, nothing erudite. Mimi Sheraton may have the up-to-the-minute word on New York's latest Szechwan hangout. Gael Greene may tell us whether the marinara sauce is hotter uptown or downtown. But millions of eaters are landing every year in Lisbon, Brussels, and Rome. Where would they be without Sheldon?

The Taxicab Rip-off

The award for the most consistent and imaginative rip-off in Europe goes to the Italian cab driver. Don't *ever* expect the correct charge from a taxi driver in Rome. In the smaller cities your prospects improve. It's not so much that the cab drivers have more integrity, it's just that they have less imagination.

In Rome, the cab drivers are clever, unscrupulous, and either articulate or hopelessly inarticulate in whichever language you are speaking. They are, in addition, on home ground and confident, and they play the rip-off game a dozen times a day. Arguing against a cab driver in Rome is an exercise in futility and frustration. *Winning* the argument is simply impossible.

There are many ways the Italian cab driver rips you off, and here they are:

1. IL SUPPLEMENTO. All taxis carry a card which indicates that if the fare is 1,000 lire, it isn't really 1,000 lire because there is a 200 lire surcharge called *il supplemento*. This is printed in a fairly official manner and it reads something like this:

1,000–1,200	Supplemento 200 lire
1,200–1,500	Supplemento 300 lire

The cab driver is adept at shoving a card under your nose at the end of the trip and shouting out, *"Supplemento!"* There is not much you can do about it because it does seem official and it's difficult to read all those numbers so quickly. So pay up.

2. LA FERIA. *La feria* means "holiday," of which there are a considerable number in Italy, particularly during tourist season. It

is almost impossible, even for an experienced traveler, to be certain that a particular day is not a holiday, especially when the driver describes the event with appropriate flag-waving, salutes, and national anthems. After all, maybe it *is* a holiday, and maybe a holiday *is* extra.

3. SUNDAY. Sunday is a *supplemento* all to itself, so first you add on *il supplemento* and then you add on Sunday, and a 1,000 lire meter becomes 1,400 lire.

4. THE EXTRA PASSENGER. This is always a *supplemento* and if there are two extra passengers the more brazen cab drivers will try for two *supplementos*. It is definitely not supposed to be a surcharge, but that is hardly of concern to the Italian cab driver.

5. BAGGAGE. Baggage is an obvious *supplemento*. The driver's rule is: Get as much as possible.

Before we proceed you may ask why *all* these devices are needed. After all, a driver cannot turn a 1,000 lire meter charge into 2,500 lire by adding on ten *supplementos*. That's true, but the driver never knows when a customer is wise to the standard rip-offs and requires a more imaginative approach. The driver needs a magic hat full of *supplementos*, one of which is certain to confuse. Confusion is victory for the cab driver and defeat for the rider. Hesitation is fatal. If you can't contest the surcharge right away and with conviction, you might as well pay it.

And incidentally, I had a cab driver who tried to turn a 1,000 lire meter charge into 2,500 lire. While we argued about it the meter kept running, so that by the time I turned aside his first five *supplementos*, it cost me a buck in meter time. Which brings us to number six.

6. THE METER ALWAYS RUNS. There is no way that a traveler, in a city for five days, can remember where the meter starts, so the Italian cab driver starts it before you enter the cab. If you are standing at the doorway of your hotel and you signal for a cab, he starts the meter. Illegal? Certainly. But try to explain it to him in Italian.

The meter also runs after the trip is completed. So while you are fumbling around with foreign coins and arguing about the *supplemento*, the charge goes up. The driver is delighted to argue because he is being paid for it.

Perhaps you think you have the answer to that one. You simply learn how to say "Stop the meter" in Italian. Forget it. The Italian cab driver is adept at understanding what he wants to understand, and few travelers are sufficiently confident of their Italian phraseology to hold their ground.

7. THE HOUR OF THE NIGHT. At a certain hour, known only to cab drivers, a "night" *supplemento* is added on. The correct hour is 10 P.M., which means that any hour after 6 P.M. is fair game.

8. THE GAS CHARGE. Everyone knows that gasoline is outrageously expensive, especially the Italian cab driver. His argument is therefore persuasive. He says, "Gasoline *supplemento.*" Who can argue? The fact is that the *supplemento* card—see number one—is intended to cover the gasoline spiral. But facts will get you nowhere with the Italian cab driver.

9. ORDERED BY TELEPHONE. If you ask your concierge to call a cab, or if you call one yourself, that's a surcharge. It's actually a legitimate one, which gives the driver a new weapon. If you challenge the *supplementos*, he becomes particularly indignant when he reaches the telephone *supplemento*. Nothing will do but to ask someone, so you ask someone. The cab driver is right, and the sanctity of the other four *supplementos* is established.

10. THE RETURN TRIP. The cab driver, delivering you to a more remote section of town, demands a surcharge for his trip back to where he found you. This is outrageous and nobody pays it. However, it allows the driver a few minutes of arguing time on the meter, and it also diverts your attention from some other *supplementos*, equally illegal but less obvious.

There you are—ten *supplementos*, and we haven't even mentioned THE AIRPORT RIP-OFF. No traveler is as vulnerable as the overseas tourist who arrives with luggage in a strange city at seven in the morning—worn out, jet-lagged, and unable to speak the language. The Italian cab driver will charge him anything.

Now that you know how you are going to be ripped off, what should you do about it? I would suggest that you do nothing. You can dispute the charge and spend your vacation fighting with cab drivers, or you can smile and lose gracefully. The important thing to remember is that 200 lire is 22¢.

It's very easy to lose sight of this. You know you're getting hustled, and you know *how* you're getting hustled. Are you going to let some cab driver take advantage of you? I hope so.

I tried it the other way. I learned all the *supplementos* and I spoke enough Italian to handle the dialogue. Every time I got into a cab I started to prepare myself for the battle. And of course there always was a battle, and I even won some of them. The fruits of my victory were 22¢, some immature satisfaction, and being tense for the next half hour. Some victory. Consider also that a cab is bringing you to some place you want to go, a restaurant or a museum perhaps. You can ruin a whole dinner if it takes you fifteen minutes to calm down after an argument with a cab driver.

Where to draw the line? At outrage, I guess. If a cab driver asks 2,500 lire for a 1,000 lire meter reading, I would give him 1,500 lire and walk out of the cab. Although that happened to me once, it is very rare. The Italian cab drivers beat you for 200 or 300 lire and that's about it. It happened to me in Rome, on a trip from the Hotel Hassler (elegant) to the Vatican, and I suppose you could argue that if an American tourist stays at the Hassler he ought to *expect* the cab drivers to invent *supplementos.*

Remember that you're on vacation; that the battleground is back in New York or Chicago; that the air fare is $1,000 round trip. Remember also that the cab driver has never been outside of Italy, while you are, in fact, the rich American. So when he demands a *supplemento feria* and it's not a holiday, remember that it's your holiday and he's hustling for a living. Smile and pay up.

Coping with the Restaurant Check

We were having dinner one evening at a small family restaurant in Rome. Mama worked in the kitchen, and Papa and two sons raced around among the tables. The result was total confusion. The soup arrived after the veal; the wine didn't arrive at all (we went up and got it); and someone at a table to our right was served our Chicken Cacciatore, while we got their Osso Buco. Actually, not a bad trade.

It's often that way in the Italian trattorias. Italy is not the most organized country in Europe, and if you wish to dine with elegance and precision, stay out of the trattorias. On the other hand, if you wish to try the best food in Europe, outside of France, Italy is where they serve it.

Anyway, one of the sons was serving us and he finally brought the check. I added it. It was wrong. So I gave it back to him and he apologized profusely. He was genuinely repentant, took it back to the kitchen to correct, and soon returned proudly with the corrected version. I added it and it was wrong again. Had I been wiser I would have shut up and paid it, but no, I returned it to him again, and he was crestfallen. By this time Papa, who was watching all the tables out of the corner of his eye, came over and asked what was wrong. When his son announced that he had twice added the check incorrectly, the father flew into a rage. He cursed the son and turned to apologize to us, then cursed the son again. His gestures were flamboyant; he blamed the mother's side four generations back; he wiped his brow, held his heart, and invoked the mercy of the pope. He also grabbed the check from his son and raced back to the kitchen, very nearly colliding with his other son, who was carrying a huge bowl of spaghetti swimming in marinara sauce. In three minutes he calmed down and returned with the corrected check. He bowed slightly and smiled, touching the curled end of his handlebar mustache. I added it. The check was wrong again.

RISTORANTE **GALEASSI**

ROMA - PIAZZA S. MARIA IN TRASTEVERE, 3 - 3a - ROMA
TELEFONO 5803775 - 5809898

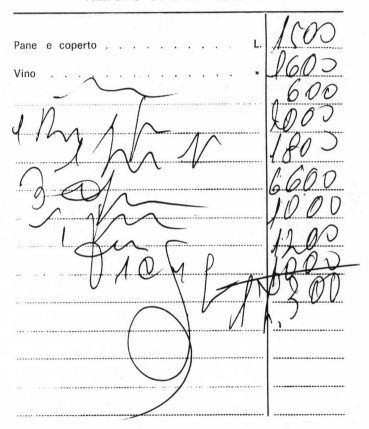

Pane e coperto . . . . L.

Vino . . . . ,,

That's Italy. Warm, friendly, lovable—disorganized, inexact, stumbling.

I point this out because getting ripped off in Italian restaurants is not really getting ripped off. They know how to cook; they just don't know how to add.

Italians don't write legibly either, so be prepared when you have dinner in Italy. There is no hope whatever that you will understand the check. For those who refuse to believe that they can be presented with a check that is indecipherable, I offer a couple of examples.

RISTORANTE AUGUSTEA
(già CAPRI)
di LUDOVICO e DOMENICO

ROMA - VIA DELLA FREZZA, 5 (Angolo Via del Corso)
Tel. 684.628 - 684.081

TUTTE LE SPECIALITA' ROMANE
— *VINI FINISSIMI* —

Il locale funziona anche dopo gli spettacoli

You will observe at once that there are three things you cannot understand: the numbers, the handwriting, and the words. How can you possibly figure out the check?

Now, how are you going to handle this? You can request an explanation for each course, and you will get it. The Italians are helpful and courteous, and not easily offended. They will explain each item, but of course they will explain it in Italian.

The most intelligent and relaxing thing is to pay the bottom line and forget about explanations. We had four people on the check that totals 22,800 lire. That's $6.30 a head, tip and taxes included. There is really no sense in having a confrontation.

Again you must consider that if you are going to concern yourself during dinner with the appearance of the check, you will certainly never enjoy dinner. You might look at it this way: In Italy dinner is both a joy and a bargain, even if you can't read the check—even if they slide in an 800 lire pasta that you never had. In other countries, England for instance, the check is a pleasure to read, until you reach the bottom line.

Taxis Are for Tourists—
Try a Motor Scooter

Travel styles are changing. At first it was twelve-cities-in-fourteen-days, but soon we were laughing at that punishment. At first it was the monument and museum route, but somehow, after a while, monuments began to look like monuments. Very soon, if the dollar does not vanish altogether, Europe will be as easy to visit as Atlantic City. So that the traveler, just a little tired of the standard itinerary, is going to want new experiences.

I'd like to talk about a new experience, but I've purposely left it for this chapter, because if you read this too early in the book, you would figure there's not much sense reading further. The "new experience" is motor scooters. You can rent one in Rome and go scootering all around town.

I should point out that it helps to know a little about how to work a scooter. Traffic patterns in strange cities can be scary even if you're in an automobile. It's worse on a scooter.

I know something about a motor scooter, because I used to drive one in college. In fact, the only accident I ever had was when my scooter was sideswiped by a 98 Oldsmobile, which wasn't supposed to be on campus anyway. I broke my wrist.

One summer Rita and I were in Rome, walking the streets and eating *gelati*, and I noticed a shop that rented motor scooters. I hadn't really thought about it before, but it sounded like an exciting thing to try. I drove the scooter up and down the block a few times, getting used to it. I was a little scared, but I wasn't going to back down now. Soon I graduated to driving around the block, and then I took off—in all directions and with no boundaries—to see Rome.

Before you say it's ridiculous, let me make two suggestions. First, if you were in Bermuda, you would probably rent a motorbike, so it can't be *that* dangerous. Second, if you can't handle a motorbike, you can certainly handle a regular bike. The same principle will apply.

There is a strange exhilaration in riding a motor scooter in Rome. You cannot get it walking. You certainly do not get it in a car or taxi. It's a sense of freedom, a feeling of being in tune with a city; of touching it in its far corners and narrow alleys. You have no plan, no sequence, no itinerary. There are no tour guides or sight-seeing books. You just drive around. In twenty minutes you are in a part of the city that tourists hardly ever get to, and suddenly you are in the center of an outdoor fruit and vegetable market. So you get off the scooter and walk around, and *this* is Rome. You buy a couple of peaches and get back on the scooter, and after another ten minutes you're going through a red-light district; not the showcase red-light district that all the tourists are taken to, but a more run-down area, shabby and seedy and a little frightening.

Ten minutes more and you're in an antique section. You seem to remember that the taxi drove around this area yesterday, but now you are *in* it. The shops have a face and a name, and you stop to look at an old brass scale in the window. If you like it you can walk inside, because you've learned enough Italian to get through any conversation that is likely to take place in the antique shop. And then you go on your way. Down the block there is a coffee shop, and it's time to call your wife and tell her that you're still alive. And *that* is exciting, because you have never used a pay phone in Italy. The cashier gives you a token and you put it in the right slot (maybe) and say very slowly to the operator, in Italian, "I'm from New York and I speak just a little Italian. Could you connect me with the Hotel Hassler?"

After the call you're elated. There is something exhilarating about a simple thing like making a pay phone call in Rome. It sounds mundane, but it is curiously exciting. For its part, the Colosseum sounds exciting, but it is curiously mundane.

It's time for a cup of coffee. So you sit at the bar and ask for *caffè* and the bartender pulls a lever on his espresso machine. There are a lot of pipes and nozzles, and he places a cup under one of them and about two inches of coffee guzzles out. Its color is almost chocolate, and there is a thin mocha head. Once you've tried it, there is no coffee anywhere that will entirely satisfy you again.

The bartender seems willing to put up with your Italian. In fact, he's really friendly and anxious to talk to someone from New York. Remember, you're in some far corner of Rome; not many Americans walk into this place, and those who do are remote and aloof because there is a language barrier. Everyone can ask, "How much?" and say, "Good afternoon," but you can do more than that.

There's a whole world waiting for you in a simple coffee shop.

You get back on the motor scooter and follow the map, moving in the approximate direction of home. You go a dozen blocks, then correct your directions and go on. You come out of one district and into another. Rome changes color before your eyes. You feel it. You sense it. You are a part of it.

I think it is something like going to a fancy French restaurant in New York when you are young and don't know your way around French restaurants. Everything is strange—the accents, the menu, the wine list. You feel as though you do not belong, and you are always on edge. But then you come back a few times and get to know things, and you feel confident that if the maître d' suggests *poulet* you will know what it is. Suddenly you are not strange; you're comfortable. It is that way in a foreign city. If you can just cross the bridge to familiarity and confidence, it is a different experience.

The average traveler is cautious. He can't rent a scooter because he worries about getting lost. He feels uncertain and stays close to his hotel in the safety of prescribed avenues and shops. But you don't have to—you are free. All of Rome is open to you, every street, every shop. It's thrilling.

The $12 Bowl of Soup

The first time I landed in Europe was at the Rome airport, and I knew that Italian money was counted in lire and that 650 lire was worth a dollar. I thought I was pretty smart. I went to the cashier's window at the airport, changed $50, hailed a cab, and set out for our hotel. When we arrived, I became frozen; all that funny-looking money in my pocket and I had to pay the driver. I got all mixed up, and I think I must have given him the equivalent of $25. Following that, I either vastly overtipped or painfully undertipped the porter who brought in our bags. It took a full hour or two until I could think in lire. Those two hours cost me both embarrassment and hard cash.

There's a better way. You can get a foreign money pack at many large American banks. You exchange ten American dollars for an assortment of the currency of the country you are visiting. And while you are flying over the Atlantic, you take out the money pack and examine the coins and bills. In half an hour you are comfortable. You know where the coins stop and the paper money begins. You know which coin serves as the conventional "quarter tip." And if the cab driver says "2,500 lire," you do not have to deposit your entire bankroll in his lap and ask him to take out the proper amount.

Here's another suggestion, but only for those who have trouble converting lire and francs into dollars. For most travelers this is not a problem, but for some, when the saleswoman in the jewelry shop says "440 francs," all mathematical functions of the brain stop working. The easy way to approach this is to arrive at a conversion table that works like this: Let's say the franc is worth 24¢; the rule for conversion is *divide by four*—four francs to the dollar.

True, that's not precise, and if you're the kind of mathematical acrobat who can divide by 4.2, go to it. But dividing by four gives you instant conversion, and when the saleswoman says "440 francs," you know it's $110. (Actually it's $105.) I'm not being casual about $5, and anytime I'm serious enough to buy something for that kind of money, I'll do the arithmetic. But it's confusing and embarrassing to do problems in long division when you are being shown a handsome shirt and comparing it to other shirts on display. It's better to be able to think fast.

The "divide by four" rule works especially well when you are window-shopping. You stop at a jewelry shop with fifty price tags in the window and you can convert them at a glance. A thousand francs? Two hundred fifty dollars. Two hundred twenty francs? Fifty-five dollars.

It is also very helpful when you ask for information. There's a tour guide camped outside your hotel, and as you leave he approaches and suggests an all-day tour of Paris for 160 francs. You would like to take the tour, but you're not sure how much that means in dollars. Divide by four.

Finally, the rule is terrific in restaurants. The waiter hands you a menu and there are seventy or eighty dishes. You could spend the entire evening figuring out the exact prices, but if you divide by four you come close enough. The menu reads, "Coq au Vin—forty francs." That's $10. Does it really matter that it's actually $9.60?

I don't think it does. You're hoping to spend a pleasant evening in a fine French restaurant. There are enough barriers already. There are enough unknowns to make you feel uncertain, even intimidated. The language is strange; the dishes are unusual. Why not make the prices easy?

Rita and I learned this through painful experience. We were at Chez Denis, that elegant restaurant (now closed) where Craig Claiborne arranged the famous $3,000 dinner for two. The owner took our order, and he was haughty in the manner of the Parisian maître d'. I didn't help matters any. I asked him for suggestions and said specifically, "Something that we are not likely to find in the French restaurants in New York." He said, "There is nothing we serve here that remotely resembles the cuisine in New York."

Rita and I asked for a few moments more to consider the menu, and somehow we came upon Lobster Bisque. I don't know why we chose it; it is hardly a soup that you would travel to Paris to try. Anyway, we checked the price. Forty-eight francs—that's right, forty-eight francs.

"How much is that?" I asked Rita.

"I think it's $4," she said. "Anyway, how much can it be for soup?"

"Right," I answered.

And we ordered Lobster Bisque. Very shortly thereafter the owner passed our table carrying a live lobster, and he smiled at us. It was then that I got out the conversion chart and figured out that forty-eight francs at 24¢ a franc wasn't $4. Naturally I blamed the whole thing on Rita.

So that night at Chez Denis we ate a $12 soup, and there's not even a dollar's worth of exaggeration.

Had we known to divide by four, we would have converted forty-eight francs instantly and wondered what the hell we were doing in a restaurant that serves $12 soups.

Incidentally, the rule works because most currencies—the franc, the mark, the escudo, the peseta—divide *into* the dollar. The lira also divides into the dollar, but you would need the math department of M.I.T. to do the calculation. (The rule is: Divide by 900.) Instead, when converting lire to dollars, drop the last digit. A restaurant check of 27,452 lire is $27.45 or $27, since these are only approximations. A 500 lire newspaper is 50¢.

It requires only a minute with each currency to construct a formula that will save you hours of uncertainty, hours of anxiety, moments of embarrassment, and probably some money.

Did You Intend to Order Octopus?

The major problem in any foreign restaurant is understanding the menu. Many restaurants with a large tourist trade will translate into English, but what do you do in the small, remote family restaurants that are really the flavor of Paris or Rome? Even if you speak the language and even if you spend considerable time in French and Italian restaurants in New York or Los Angeles, the dishes in Paris and Rome sound different. And it's the different ones that you want to try. You can have Coq au Vin and Veal Parmigiana at home.

There's a solution to this problem: an inexpensive pocket book called *Eating in Eight Languages* by Wilma George, published by Stein and Day. This book has, in alphabetical order, almost every dish on a European menu, so that if the specialty of the day is *calamari*, and you don't think you're quite ready to try squid, you're properly advised.

We don't like to carry along even a pocket book, so we cut out the pages of the country we are visiting and we carry them constantly for reference. When we open the menu I read the names of the dishes that sound strange, and Rita finds them in the guide. It takes about three minutes.

At first we were embarrassed about opening our guide-to-translate-the-menu. It seemed so unsophisticated. We used to open the guide surreptitiously and close it as soon as we sighted the waiter. We also used to open it inside the menu so that we could be observed reading intently, when in fact we were translating from Italian to English.

It is amazing how easily the tourist is intimidated. Here we were, doing a perfectly normal thing, trying to figure out the dishes on a foreign menu, and we were trying to do it secretly. After a while it occurred to us that it was not only not a crime, but that it showed interest and concern for what the restaurant was serving. So we held our guide right out in front, and when the waiter asked if we needed help, we answered that we just wanted to be sure we understood all the interesting dishes that the chef was preparing.

Sometimes the waiter will bring the menu in English as soon as he sees that we are translating, but we always ask to be left with the regular menu, preferring to negotiate the problem the best way we can.

Never Make a Reservation in Your Own Name

I have a reservation at Colline Emiliane, one of Rome's most interesting small restaurants. I called it in myself this afternoon, speaking very slowly.

It's seven o'clock. I arrive at the restaurant. "Signor Bernstein," I say. "Dinner reservation for two."

The owner looks at his reservations book, looks up at me, looks at the book again. "I'm sorry," he says, "we have no reservation in your name."

"You must have. I made the reservation this afternoon. Bernstein. Leonard Bernstein."

He looks up and shrugs—not impolitely, not without sympathy (the Italians are always sympathetic). He simply doesn't have the reservation.

I lean over the edge of his book, a bit more assertive than I have the right to be. There's no Bernstein listed. Wait a minute—there is *something* listed. It looks like "Borensitin." I point to it.

"Ah, BER-EN-SI-TINE!" he laughs. *"Buona sera, buona sera."*

The moral: Never make a reservation in your own name.

Over the years, in many European countries, I have been making reservations in the name of Mr. Bernstein, and when I arrive at the restaurant and announce my name they advise that they have no reservation. The Europeans aren't sloppy; it's just that most countries can't deal with a name like Bernstein. Remember that English pronunciation is strange to anyone with even a remote sense of logic. We have words like "thorough" that any orderly language would spell "thoro." And most languages in Europe are orderly; they spell words the way they sound. And they can't spell "Bernstein."

It was only after many disappointments that I evolved the system of peeking at the reservations book and trying to figure out which name they wrote when I called. After all, I did make the reservation and they did write down something. The problem was to find it.

After some embarrassment and unkind words from restaurant owners and maître d's who felt, not without some justification, that I should not be examining their reservations book, I found a simple solution. I make reservations in the name of Mr. Leonardo, and I pronounce it LAY-O-NARDO. Leonardo is a name that Euro-

peans are familiar with. It is a common first name; it is spelled as it sounds; and of course there was Leonardo da Vinci. Even in France and Denmark, where they decidedly do not pronounce words as they are spelled, Leonardo is Leonardo.

Consider your own name. If it is basically phonetic, most Europeans can handle it. Robert Costello, for example, can reserve under his own name. Robert Weickert would be wise to make his reservations as Mr. Roberto. You should also consider the country: In Germany, a Bernstein can reserve under Bernstein. It takes a bit of thought to evaluate whether your name is easily translated. Here are a few examples and some recommendations:

ARTHUR SCHLESINGER.	Try Mr. AR-TU-RO.
ALI MACGRAW.	Ali is easy; MacGraw is impossible. Say Miss A-LI.
RICHARD SCHWARTZ.	Use Mr. RI-CAR-DO. Don't even consider trying Schwartz.
EDWARD KENNEDY.	Kennedy is not difficult, especially since the name has been in European headlines so often. Nevertheless, if you want to try the system, say Mr. ED-WAR-DO.
EDWARD KOCH.	*Definitely* Mr. Edwardo.
BARBARA WALTERS.	Say Miss BAR-BAR-A, and roll the r's a little.

There is a school of thought that suggests that "Mr. Leonardo" can be improved upon. They say to use "Dr. Leonardo"—the theory being that a doctor commands a little more respect than a mister. I suppose that's true, but I have a friend who tried it, and yes, he did get a rather nice table. However, about halfway through his linguine with clam sauce the maître d' rushed over to his table and told him that they needed his help immediately. A diner at another table had just passed out.

The Bitterest-Tasting Stuff in the World

After you've mastered the menus of Paris and Rome, indulging in sauces and spices, strawberry tarts and liqueurs, you may find that your stomach has not kept up with your culinary spirit. Around the third day the stomach revolts, having been assaulted not only by exotic flavors and excessive portions, but by the products of a foreign soil.

Generally the alarm system sounds softly at first, with a dull ache or a feeling of fullness. But if you don't act at once, your entire restaurant itinerary is threatened.

There is a solution to gastric insurrection, and I am about to reveal it. I have the feeling that it might be the most important thing you will learn from this book. How many people, on vacation in Paris, would not give their kingdom for a simple and effective solution to upset stomach?

The solution is Fernet-Branca. Fernet-Branca is an aperitif, and is sold at most of the bars in Europe. It is described on the label as "a bitter stimulant to the appetite." No one will argue that it is bitter. It is probably the bitterest-tasting stuff in the world. Whether or not it is a stimulant to the appetite is irrelevant, because nobody is going to suffer through even a few sips of Fernet-Branca in order to stimulate the appetite.

Fernet-Branca seems to work by paralyzing the stomach. The nerves around the stomach wall get desensitized as though injected with novocaine, and no longer convey their distress to the rest of the body. How does Fernet-Branca accomplish this? I'm not really certain, and I'm not sure that I want to know. It contains some exotic medicinals: aloes, gentian, zedoary, cinchona, calumba, galangal, rhubarb, bryonia, angelica, myrrh, chamomile, saffron, and peppermint oil. That sounds like enough to paralyze a charging rhinoceros.

Fernet-Branca is not well known in the United States (although many bars serve it), but the European bartenders are knowledgeable about it. They also know why you are ordering it, and occasionally they will suggest ways to make it taste a little better. This means that it will only taste terrible, which is the most you can hope for from Fernet-Branca.

The world's expert bartender on Fernet-Branca is Alarico Pérez, at the Palace Hotel in Madrid. Señor Pérez has some secret recipes to make the drink almost palatable, and I'm passing them along. It may be that Señor Pérez is the most important person to see in all Madrid. He certainly saved my trip.

Alarico serves the aperitif over ice with a few drops of peppermint. It does take the sting out of it. However, expecting ice and peppermint to pacify Fernet-Branca would be to expect the Boy Scouts to stop the Third Army. Another solution is usually needed, and Alarico suggests that you mix it with Coke syrup. Coke syrup is said to be good for the stomach anyway, and it is pretty heavy stuff. Alarico has it on hand just for this reason, and it reduces Fernet-Branca to tasting barely palatable.

Anyone about to try this aperitif should read the label first. I don't want to recommend medicines, and Fernet-Branca comes close. There is a caution about a laxative effect (in the event of overdose), and of course not all stomach disorders are indigestion. So pay attention.

But one day, after the fiery sauces of Italy or the sensuous custard pastries of France, that green monster will crawl up under your gills. Forget about Alka-Seltzer and all that other kid stuff and take a sip of Fernet-Branca. It will overhaul your digestive tract and get you right back on the road.

Don't Waste Time Shopping

I'd like to bring up a sensitive subject: Buying presents for friends and relatives. My suggestion is, *don't*.

You will at once accuse me of being callous and inconsiderate, but I'm not going to back down. Buying presents is one of the biggest traveling mistakes that I have made.

There are exceptions. If I'm walking along the Via Veneto in Rome and I spot an absolutely perfect gift for a particular friend, I buy it; no problem. The problem begins when I take with me to Europe a long list of presents that I *must* buy. And let's be honest; that's the way it happens, isn't it? We all feel that there are friends and relatives to whom we are *expected* to bring a gift.

Often it is even worse than that. Occasionally friends will tell you what they want you to bring back. Usually it is a reasonable request. There is this Florentine gold pin that sells for $100 in Chicago, and costs only $50 in Florence. Since you're going to be in Florence anyway, why not pick it up? Your friend is not asking that you pay for it.

I knew this was a mistake when I arrived in Florence carrying just such a request in the back of my mind. Here I was in one of the world's great cities, free to visit the museums and restaurants, and what was I thinking about? Looking around for a Florentine gold pin to save $50.

Of course, I didn't have to get it. The understanding was that I would buy it if I saw it. But it doesn't work that way. It's on your back like a piece of baggage. You want to get it out of the way, and until you do, you're not free. Before you know it, you are planning your day to include one or two jewelry shops that you had no intention of visiting. You're spending $200 a day to tour Europe, and you're being bothered by a $50 piece of jewelry. It's a mistake.

You may reasonably reply, "But it's fun to shop for presents for people when you visit Florence." I can't argue with that. If that's what you prefer to do, do it. But if you really don't *prefer* to do it, and are just doing it because it's the social thing, it's time for courage. It's time to put your foot down. You get two weeks during the whole year to visit Italy, and you have a right to be a little selfish.

Let's take this matter of presents one step further. I think we make a mistake looking for presents for *ourselves*. I remember very clearly a cruise we took through the Caribbean. The cruise ship stopped for an afternoon or a day at Barbados. The tourists left the ship, spent the day on the island, and returned to the ship in the evening. Now I ask you, what did we do on the island of Barbados during the day? Did we tour it, searching out its charm and color? Did we try to get a feeling for the island, for its culture or its people? Did we even use the opportunity to do some scuba diving? We did not. What one-day tourists do on the island of Barbados is to rush to the liquor store and buy six bottles of Grand Marnier at half price.

I'm absolutely sure of this, because I was one of those tourists. The boat landed in Barbados and we all raced to the liquor store. I wasn't one of the first to get there, so I was pretty far back in line. Yes, there I was, spending a thousand for a one-week Caribbean tour, and I was spending my afternoon standing in line to buy liquor.

It's true, you can save some money. Maybe you save $30 on a six-pack of Grand Marnier. But isn't there something better to do on the island of Barbados? If not, why are we taking the cruise?

One last thing. This works both ways. Never, absolutely never, ask a friend to bring back one of those marvelous cable-knit sweaters that they sell in the shops in Lisbon. Your friend can't say no, and if you consider that your request may be multiplied by five other friends and relatives, you are really sending him on a shopping tour.

Bosoms and Mustaches: A Story of the Airlines

It is 7:30 in the morning, and I leave my house to catch a nine o'clock flight from La Guardia to Harrisburg. Plenty of time. But there's an accident on the expressway and I finally race to the airline counter at 9:15—hoping.

"The Harrisburg flight!" I shout. "Has it left?"

"Left on schedule," says the attendant.

I turn away, frustrated and disappointed. I'm supposed to attend an important business meeting in Harrisburg, and there's no other morning flight out. The day is ruined. I start to walk back to my car, but it occurs to me—I'm not sure why—that the departure gate is only about a two-minute walk. So I go to the gate and there's the plane, just in the process of boarding.

I have a theory about airlines. I believe that in the air, like the bald eagle and the condor, they are things of beauty and efficiency. But on the ground, also like the great birds, they stumble along.

I have never had trouble with an airline in flight. A bumpy ride perhaps, or a cold meal, but remarkable order and speed of deliverance. Indeed, considering that an aircraft departs and arrives every minute at the major airports of the world, we have incredibly few mishaps in flight.

I suspect that is because the airplane is a marvel of engineering, but marvelous only in its element. The engineering serves little purpose on the ground, and the airline becomes an awkward collection of systems, data, and people.

And so, I have three survival suggestions for dealing with airlines, but not one related to a plane in flight. If you make it into the sky, chances are you'll be safe and comfortable, and that's what really matters, isn't it? But until you make it into the sky, prepare for the worst.

1. AIRLINE INFORMATION MUST BE CHECKED. You call an airline; they have no space. Do you delay the trip? Of course not. When an airline reports that it has no space, remember that this is the voice of a computer. Computers talk to other computers across thousands of miles, and sometimes they don't get along with each other. Even if they do get along, computers are only contraptions made of red and green wires, running through tunnels and along electrical highways. Sometimes the traffic on the highways gets backed up and the information doesn't run through at its usual million-miles-an-hour pace. Anyway, I *think* that's what goes wrong, because I have been told "No space available" by one computer, and when I call back five minutes later I'm on the flight. Certainly, there could have been cancellations in five minutes, but it happens all too often for me to believe that it is not computer idiosyncracy.

It is remarkable how few travelers check their tickets. People will check tickets to a basketball game and to the theater, but airline tickets somehow fall into the category of electric bills. We glance at them, but that's about all.

Airline tickets are written either by people or computers, and it has not yet been determined which make more mistakes. If you don't want to find that the plane left yesterday, check your ticket. Check the date and time of departure, the flight number, and the number of people your ticket covers. If you arrive at the airport with your wife and two kids and the ticket reads three, your insistence that you made the reservation for four is not a winning argument.

So, reconfirm. Even if you don't have to, reconfirm. You never know what error may come to light when the reservation is being reviewed.

Finally, if you are traveling outside of the United States, absolutely assume that something will go wrong. Even if your tickets are checked by a concierge, do not hesitate to call or to stop at an airline office and confirm. France and Italy may offer delights that cannot be found between New York and California, but one thing they do not offer is more dependable airline information.

2. NEVER TAKE NO FOR AN ANSWER. Never accept, "I'm sorry, we don't fly to Albuquerque, and none of the other airlines have flights going out to Albuquerque this evening." Hang up and try one of the

other airlines. There has to be a way to get to Albuquerque. It's one chance in three that the next airline either has a flight that evening or knows who does. Even if they don't, they are likely to suggest that you fly to Dallas and connect from Dallas to Albuquerque. Remember, reservations people are just people. If you catch one three minutes before quitting time and he's backed up with work, he may be less imaginative about the routes to Albuquerque than another person who hasn't taken a call in fifteen minutes and is dying of boredom.

I am reminded of a ski trip our family took to Park City, Utah. Rita and the three children took a limousine from our home to Kennedy Airport. I came straight from New York City. We were scheduled out on a six o'clock flight to Salt Lake City, but at three in the afternoon it started to snow. All the parkways became hopelessly clogged with skidding automobiles, and it took us three hours to get to the airport. We arrived at 6:30 and the flight had already left. Why do the flights leave on time on the worst days of the year, while on the nicest days they are always half an hour late?

Anyway, there we were, five of us with skis, boots, poles, duffel bags, and parkas. We couldn't get on the flight and we couldn't get back home, because by now all the roads were completely blocked off. We were frustrated, aggravated, and sullen, and faced with the prospect of spending the night in Kennedy Airport.

There was another airline that had a nine o'clock flight, so I went to the reservations counter to see if I could switch the tickets. Our tickets, however, called for an excursion rate and included the round-trip flight, the lodging, and even the ski lift tickets. It was a single package from a single airline, and when I suggested a change in airlines for the flight out, I was offered the conventional "It can't be done."

"Now wait a minute," I argued. "You mean to say that during the worst snowstorm of the winter, when every road to the airport is virtually blocked off, you can't make an exception on an excursion ticket? I thought all the airlines cooperated with each other. You have empty space on your nine o'clock. Why should it matter if we take a different airline out?"

"The only difference is the fare. Your excursion fare is based on a round trip with one airline."

"So you're saying that unless I want to scrap my entire saving for five people on the excursion rate, I have to wait around the airport until tomorrow evening at six o'clock?"

"You don't have to wait around the airport, but you do have to wait for tomorrow's six o'clock flight."

"But we can't get home from the airport. The roads are all blocked."

That observation went uncontested, but no solution was forthcoming.

So I asked Rita to keep an eye on the reservations counter just in case that clerk went out for dinner and another took his place. Never assume that two clerks will agree that something can't be done. Meanwhile, I went to another airline that had an eleven o'clock flight out to Chicago with a transfer to Salt Lake City. I caught the clerk eating a grilled cheese on rye with bacon.

"Pretty good sandwich," I ventured.

"Yeah, on a night like this I'm lucky they let me grab a sandwich altogether."

"Sure, I know how you feel. We just got to the airport and we missed our flight to Utah. We can't get out to Utah and we can't get back to our house. Say, what's doing on your eleven o'clock to Chicago with a transfer to Salt Lake City?"

"Oh, you can get on that. How many are you?"

So I waited for him to take another bite of the sandwich and handed him the tickets, and of course he tells me it can't be done at the excursion rate. But he's an understanding guy and it's a night for mercy, so somehow he figures out a way to do it and we're off.

Is that unethical? I don't know, maybe so. This is not a time for ethics. The choice is to sleep over on the marble floor of Kennedy Airport or to find some way to get the hell out of there. And at eleven we were on the plane.

Meanwhile, at the nine o'clock counter, the clerk who said it couldn't be done was still standing around looking mean and surly. I was tempted to tell him about the clerk at the other counter and to hand him a grilled cheese sandwich, but I wasn't brave enough.

The rule stands: Never take no for an answer.

3. FIND A NICE RESERVATIONS CLERK. This rule is quite important but is rarely given proper consideration. It is my experience that every time I check in at an airline counter something is wrong. The plane is canceled or I have too much luggage, or they won't carry skis unless they're wrapped a certain way, or something. The situation requires a thoughtful, cooperative clerk, so make sure you get in line in front of one.

I always size up the personnel before I get in line. If there are male clerks, I look for one with a mustache. Mustaches are always a positive sign. Beware, however, of a very thin or narrow mustache. That's bad news. You want a full, bushy mustache that fairly spreads across the face. If it curls at the ends, consider that a plus. Mustaches are well known to be sensitive in times of crisis.

If the clerk is a woman, I lean toward an ample bosom. Ample bosoms are kind and considerate. But be certain that you understand what I mean. "Ample" does not mean large and shapely. *Playboy* bosoms may be delightful in the centerfold, but they tend to be short-tempered behind airline counters. "Ample" means full and abundant, like Aunt Martha or Mother Earth.

There are mean people and nice people in the world, and we all believe that we can tell one from the other by looking at them. Call it first impressions or body language—it doesn't matter. The fact is that when you see a person for the first time you form an instant impression. More often than not you are correct, because nice people send out nice signals. They smile, they move with certain rhythm. Mean people scowl and their movements are abrupt. You can tell. You've been telling all your life.

Some of these nice people and mean people naturally work at airline counters, and when you check in you have a choice. So do a quick mustache and bosom study. You will find that when the flight to Albuquerque is canceled, someone will spend enough time explaining the other possibilities.

Thus ends my story of the airlines; it's certain to be contested by airlines personnel who will claim that computers can't make errors because they have engineering safeguards. Who, I wonder, builds in those engineering safeguards? In any case, I can't dwell on this. I have to check my department store statement, which has $27.49 charged for an item that is not mine. I called a vice-president, but he said, "We can't get it out of the computer."

I expect also to hear from offended groups who believe that mustaches and certainly bosoms have nothing to do with personalities. Of course I can't prove my contention without taking a survey, which could lead to considerable legal difficulties. I can only tell you that those who refuse to recognize the obvious get the worst service at the airline counters.

Finally, I expect to hear from some Airlines Industry Research Service that among 2,678,426 tickets written last year, only three were written incorrectly. I don't have the scientific data to contest their facts, but what I'd like to know is: How come I got all three?

When the Airlines Go on Strike

I'd like to tell you about my great (and only) airlines triumph, a feat of daring and ingenuity. Well, maybe more brashness than daring, and certainly more accident than ingenuity.

We had spent two weeks in Israel, and now it was time to go home. Reports of a strike at Lod Airport circulated freely around Jerusalem, but nobody seemed certain of the situation. We packed our bags and drove west from Jerusalem toward Tel Aviv. The airport is between the two cities. All five of us were there, Rita and I and our children, Laura, Audrey, and Larry; five very tired travelers carrying twice as much luggage as we needed.

We unloaded at the airport and walked inside. It was a mass of humanity—faces from all corners of the world, none of them happy. The strike was on. The airport looked like Washington's troops at Valley Forge: people huddled together, luggage strewn all over the place; some people sleeping on the floor, using backpacks for pillows. It was all confusion and chaos, with no one able to supply reliable information. Only one thing was certain: Some of the people had been waiting as long as two days.

The reservations counters were unapproachable. The lines were fifty deep. Generally the report seemed to be that El Al, the Israeli airline, was on strike, but that British Airways was still flying out. Of course everyone, for the last two days, had switched over to British Airways, so they were booked solid. We were reserved on El Al.

A scene like this drives a man to desperate measures. I searched around the airport and noted that behind each reservations counter there was a door that apparently led to headquarters. There's nothing secret about that; you'll notice that same door behind the counters at Kennedy Airport or O'Hare. Of course nobody goes through those doors except airlines personnel. You couldn't if you wanted to; the counter separates personnel from travelers.

It will be difficult to picture the next scene unless you imagine the swarm of people milling around, pushing and shoving, irritated and confused. The counters were surrounded, and often there was no personnel behind them. After all, there was no need to check anybody in.

There was a door behind one of the counters that seemed approachable, and I sort of allowed myself to be pushed in that direction. I figured that if I went through the door and got caught by security police, I could blame the pushing and shoving. I'm not even sure why I wanted to go through the door. It was a door, that's all; it led somewhere. And anywhere was better than where we were.

I opened the door and slipped through. I was in a long, narrow corridor. No one was there. Along the sides of the corridor were offices with official titles stenciled in black and gold letters against the windows. And inside each office were groups of people engaged, one would presume, in some kind of airlines business. Not, however, in the business of getting 10,000 travelers up in the sky.

It was amazing. I was just walking along the corridor. Nobody was stopping me. Nobody was asking me what I was doing there. Maybe they assumed that anyone walking around such an unlikely place had to be airlines personnel.

I finally walked past a door that said British Airways, and I could see that inside there was a large round table with about seven men in official airline attire sitting around. The fact that I had not yet been apprehended made me heady. I opened the door. If they pulled guns on me, I was prepared to say I got lost in the crowd and ended up here. It was a thin excuse, but these were not ordinary airport conditions.

I stepped inside and one of the uniforms said, "Can I help you?"

Can I help you? Would you believe that? Didn't they want to know what the hell I was doing there?

"Well yes, actually, you can help me. I have reservations on El Al to New York for a family of five, and El Al seems to be on strike. I was wondering whether I could switch to British Airways."

"Sure, we can handle that. The next plane goes out in two hours. It makes a stop in Zurich and London, and then on to New York. Is that all right?"

I almost couldn't resist asking why, with 10,000 frenzied people in the airport, the flight was not overflowing. But discretion won out; I didn't ask. I handed him the tickets and that was that.

I walked back down the corridor and out the same door, and found Rita and the children. I had to walk them outside the terminal, because if anyone overheard the story I would have been torn to shreds.

"You'll never believe this," I said.

At just about this time, friends of ours, a family of seven, arrived at the airport, also scheduled for the El Al New York flight. They had already sized up the situation—no flights out. Either set up camp for a long wait or return to the hotel in Jerusalem. They asked what we were doing.

"We're on the British Airways six o'clock flight to New York."

"That's impossible. There are people sitting around here for two days."

So I went back outside the terminal. "Jack, I know you're not going to believe me, but you walk right through that door at the side of the British Airways counter, and you'll find yourself in a long, narrow corridor . . ."

"Come on, Leonard."

"Jack, listen to me. You want to spend two nights sleeping on the floor? What have you got to lose?"

So Jack slipped through the same door and we didn't see him again for about twenty minutes, during which time his wife, Harriet, assumed he was being questioned by the Israeli Secret Service. But Jack emerged waving seven tickets in the air, at which point I was certain that three extremely tough-looking Turks were going to pound him to smithereens and grab the tickets.

Don't ask me how it worked. I don't know, and I remained too scared to ask. If the airlines say it is impossible, I don't mind a bit. I have Jack as proof.

Am I recommending that you walk through strange doors at airports? No, I'm not. And I imagine, with today's security regulations, that you probably *would* end up in a dark room with the Secret Service.

All I'm saying, and I'm not saying it with great conviction, is that airlines are marvelous up in the sky, but on the ground anything can happen and probably will. You can make things a little bit easier if you keep your eyes open and assume that nothing is impossible.

Remembrance of Things Pasta

It may be possible to try twenty-six different pasta dishes at twenty-six different restaurants in thirteen days, but we didn't quite manage it. The drive from Siena to Perugia somehow threw us off schedule. We did, however, manage twenty-five.

It was not an attempt at a listing in the Guinness *Book of World Records*. We just ate pasta because we love pasta, and nowhere in the world can it possibly be better. We had a salad or antipasto for lunch, followed by a Spaghetti con Vongole. And by dinner time we were ready for a Tagliatelle alla Strascinata as a first course.

Pasta is a first course in Italy. It may or may not be preceded by a soup or antipasto—that's optional—but it is always followed by a *secondo*. The second course is veal or fish or fowl, and that may be accompanied by *contorni* (vegetables) and finished off with a Zuppa Inglese and espresso. One is startled by the amount of food that the Italian consumes during dinner, and it only begins to make sense when you realize that dinner is a three-hour affair and the evening activity. So leisurely is the evening dinner that the Italian orders it course by course, completing one course before even ordering the next. After all, an Italian will explain, how can you know what you want after the pasta until you finish the pasta? And so the Italian lingers over his ravioli, talking and drinking the house wine, and doesn't even consider the next course—doesn't even consider if there will *be* a next course, although somehow a plate of something or other always seems to appear. It's a lovely way to have dinner, and once we learned it we always ordered that way, although we had to be a bit firm with the waiter, who, not unreasonably, expected Americans to order like Americans.

It might have been this lingering pace that spread dinner out between eight and eleven, or it may have been the Frascatis and Chiantis, served generously out of giant house bottles. Or it may have been the pace of vacation time when the body engine stops racing, and the heartbeat changes from a type A to type B. But somehow, regardless of pasta-for-lunch, by dinner time the appetite was raging, and another pasta seemed irresistible.

It seems a sacrilege to rate twenty-five pastas, but that's what I found myself doing. It didn't start that way; it was just a question of scribbling some idle notes. But then I started to give out stars, and I was hooked. This ravioli deserved two stars, but then I could hardly give that *bucatini* less than three. And that spaghetti last night—three stars at least, if not four or five.

When the list grew to fifteen dishes, it became even more interesting. A new pasta—*taglierini*. Marvelous. Where does it belong? Can it possibly replace number two? Could it be the best of all?

How delightful to dwell on the problem! How wonderful to anticipate where tonight's pasta might rate! Pure indolence; pure indulgence. The mind unplugs itself from the electrical currents of business, from the hypertensions of investments and negotiations, and begins to consider whether the Spaghetti con Vongole is better at Giggi Fazi or Pierluigi il Fagiolaro.

And so I present the five best pastas between Rome and Florence, including Spello, Spoleto, Siena, Perugia, and San Gimignano. Of course I could present the entire twenty-five, and it would be no sin, because the twenty-fifth pasta would still be number one or number two in New York or San Francisco.

The single best pasta I had in Italy—which is to say, the single best pasta anywhere—was the Tagliatelle Paglia e Fieno al Tartufo, served at Mamma Gina's in Florence. The restaurant is on Borgo San Jacopo, just a few minutes' walk from the Ponte Vecchio. The dish is made of green and yellow linguine sprinkled generously with white truffles, a rare and expensive delicacy found in Italy during the fall and early winter. The white truffles only remotely resemble the black; they are pungent and musty, with a flavor and odor reminiscent of ripe Liederkranz. I know of no other food or spice like white truffles. The gathering of the white truffles is a celebration in Italy—for good reason.

The dish is extremely expensive by pasta standards, costing 6,000 lire or about $6.70. A standard pasta at Mamma Gina's or anywhere else might be $2.50.

The pasta-with-white-truffles stands apart because aside from being simply delicious, there is no other dish quite so unusual and innovative. (Trattoria Mamma Gina, Borgo San Jacopo 37. Telephone: 296009)

Number two was more difficult to decide, but goes to the Spaghetti con Vongole (tiny clams) at Giggi Fazi in Rome. There is no American-Italian equivalent of this dish, because in America the clams are minced. The Italians use the word *veraci* (real) on the menu to indicate the use of tiny clams, thumbnail size, which are cooked and served right in the pasta. If you arrive at Giggi Fazi early, the waiter may pick out the clam shells, but it hardly matters. By any standard this is an incredible pasta.

Giggi Fazi is another restaurant that's easy to find. It is just off the Via Veneto, and it's not the worst idea to finish dinner without dessert or coffee and stroll the Via, picking up a *gelato* here and an espresso there. (Giggi Fazi, Via Lucullo 22. Telephone: 464045)

Fontanella in Rome, not far from the Piazza del Popolo, serves a Pappardelle al Sugo di Lepre, which translates rather badly into spiral-shaped noodles in a sauce made from the meat—and who knows what else—of the hare. It is a rich, gamy sauce that is unusual by American standards. Many restaurants in Italy serve it, and it is a delightful change from the tomato and meat sauce pastas we are so familiar with. Try the dish with a heavy wine like a Barolo, or a Chianti Riserva. Anything much lighter will fail to stand up to the richness of the sauce. (La Fontanella, Largo Fontanella di Borghese 86. Telephone: 783849)

The fourth-place pasta award goes to Spaghetti al Moro at the restaurant Al Moro, only a few minutes' walk from the Fontana di Trevi in Rome. You needn't remember to order the dish because the waiter comes over and says, "You want to start with Spaghetti al Moro." There is a certain finality to his suggestion and you accept it, although not without thinking that he should have offered more choices. The pasta arrives perfectly *al dente*, although one's first reaction is disappointment, because "al Moro" appears to be nothing more imaginative than a tomato sauce. The magic is in the taste, however, and nothing will do except to try it. (Al Moro, Vicolo delle Bollette 13. Telephone: 783495)

Fifth place belongs to a marvelous restaurant in the town of Spello, about 100 miles north of Rome. Spello is worth a stop on the drive from Rome to Florence, both to dine at Il Molino and to see the Pinturicchio frescoes in the church of Santa Maria Maggiore, just a stroll from the restaurant. The pasta to try is Tagliatelle alla Strascinata, which is served in—don't be deterred by this—a bean sauce. Of course the pasta is a first course; the specialty of the restaurant is a dish called Pinturicchio Oscar, which is not to be missed. (Il Molino, Via Cavour 24. Telephone: 65305)

Alas, to award only five medals among the twenty-five pastas is like choosing the five best paintings in the Uffizi. Furthermore, on a different day, in a different mood, it would be altogether possible to choose five others. The joy is in the search; the excitement is in the journey.

Traveling Free

The best way to travel is to travel free, and it is being done all the time. You only need some skill and some courage, mostly the latter.

Every twenty minutes or so a cruise ship leaves New York harbor, and it is the consuming passion of cruise directors to crowd into every waking hour an absolute fireworks of instruction and entertainment. So if you can instruct in yoga or bridge or Szechwan cooking, you can travel free. You have to understand that the cruise director cannot always get Charles Goren to teach bridge or James Beard to teach cooking. There's only one Charles Goren, and there are lots of cruise ships. Besides, you probably can't get Charles Goren to teach bridge for the price of a round-trip ticket, so you have to set your sights a little lower.

Now who will teach bridge for the price of a free cruise? I will, and you will. Perhaps you will point to a talent deficiency in bridge, but don't let that stop you. Just ask yourself what you *can* teach. You surely can teach something.

My friend Marvin is an accountant. Now certainly that does not suggest a form of entertainment terribly in demand on cruise ships. But Marvin was looking around among his friends who were traveling free, and he decided there ought to be something an accountant could teach that would not put people immediately to sleep.

Finally he decided that a lot of cruise ships sail in March when everybody is thinking about income taxes and how to avoid paying them, and Marvin decided to offer a course in How to Write Off Your Cruise. He did suggest strenuously that if any of the ideas sound appealing, a person should first have a long talk with his accountant.

I'm passing along Marvin's idea because it demonstrates how to turn a liability into an asset. Nobody could have been less likely to travel free than Marvin, and yet he found a way.

The tax law, simply stated, says that any expenses incurred in a legitimate business venture are deductible from your income. Therefore, if a legitimate business venture requires that you take a cruise, the cruise is deductible in the same way that a business lunch is deductible. Of course, the business must be serious. You can't say that you are thinking about investing in French wines and therefore have to visit France. If that were the case, every traveler would be suddenly thinking about investing in French wines.

However, if you had a serious investment in a French vineyard and you derived a substantial income from your investment (or even if you suffered a loss), you are entitled to pay reasonable attention to your investment. Which leads to idea number one.

Develop a serious investment in a French vineyard, preferably near Cannes or St. Tropez. After all, the law doesn't require that you invest in Bordeaux. *Where* you invest is your business. And certainly, if you own a vineyard near Cannes, you can't just let the grapes grow all over the place. You have to see to it that they are pruned and fertilized and pressed. Furthermore, it's not your fault that the grapes grow in the summertime, when the sun and the beaches on the French coast are particularly inviting. You couldn't be expected to visit your grapes in the wintertime, when there aren't any grapes growing. So there you are: You *have to* visit your investment. And what if, after a hard day at the vineyard, you relax for an hour or two and watch the bikinis at St. Tropez? Got it?

Bikinis lead to idea number two: *Manufacture cruise wear.* A manufacturer of any product has the right, as a normal business expense, to research his market. A designer of expensive dresses might have to travel to Paris every year to attend the fashion shows. A manufacturer of ski jackets might have to wander the slopes of Sun Valley or Sugarbush. It follows, therefore, that a cruise wear manufacturer would have to spend time researching *his* market, and where else can you research cruise wear better than on a cruise?

While you are researching, it is wise to remember that the best place to observe is from the deck chairs on the sunny side—right?

Idea number three is a winner and a credit to Marvin's imagination. Marvin says you could deduct the cost of the cruise if you had a serious interest in *buying the ship*. He says you couldn't be expected to go around buying ships without seeing them in action anymore than you could buy a pajama factory without looking at the sewing machines, or a restaurant without tasting the food. Not bad, Marvin. Marvin says, of course, that you have to be a real ship buyer; you have to have credentials. Otherwise all 900 passengers would be buying the ship.

You may feel that buying a ship or two is a large price to pay for deducting a cruise, but I take that as a very negative and defeatist attitude.

The next idea you probably are familiar with, because it is already being done in a different way: *Hold a convention aboard a ship*. Certainly conventions are deductible business expenses, because there are conferences and lectures and everybody learns new techniques and generally improves their professional competence. Never mind that the lectures take place between 9:30 and 10:00 in the morning, and everybody dashes out to the swimming pool for the rest of the day. You can learn a lot of new techniques between 9:30 and 10:00.

Now, where do these conventions take place, I ask you? In Baltimore or Kansas City? Of course not. It's very hard to learn new techniques in Baltimore and Kansas City. Conventions take place in the Virgin Islands, where they have laboratories and the latest equipment—the very center of intellectual ferment. So why not a convention on a cruise ship?

Marvin hastens to point out that under the 1976 Tax Reform Act the IRS takes a dim view of lectures between 9:30 and 10:00. They have demanded—although only for foreign conventions— that at least six hours a day be *scheduled business activities*. I wonder what the golf club manufacturers have to say about that!

I think it is most inconsiderate, and demonstrates a total lack of understanding. What is the sense of going to a convention if you have to listen to the lectures?

Nevertheless, that's the rule, although there is always the possibility of getting friendly with the guy who takes attendance.

There is also the question of whether a cruise to Bermuda constitutes a *foreign convention*. Marvin says he will not offer an interpretation here until he has examined some IRS rulings, although I must say this seems unduly conservative on his part.

Conventions aboard cruise ships will probably make the luxury liners a few million, and Marvin says I shouldn't give the idea

away without first arranging for part of the action. That's the way accountants think, and it may explain why all accountants live in the suburbs, while most writers are starving to death in the inner cities.

Idea number five is quick and easy to digest: *Become a painter of ocean scenes.* There have been painters who specialized in a certain subject matter. Degas painted ballet. Gauguin painted Tahiti. I daresay that if Gauguin were painting today and his paintings were bringing a few hundred thousand, as they do, he could reasonably claim that a trip to Tahiti was a legitimate expense.

On this point I challenged Marvin immediately. "Granted that an artist's subject matter is a legitimate expense," I said, "that doesn't mean he has to take an expensive cruise to find his ocean. Why couldn't he just hire a rowboat?"

Marvin considered me with disdain. "First of all, how would you set up an easel in a rowboat? Second, how would you paint with the rowboat bouncing among the waves? Third of all, who would *take* a rowboat out in the ocean? The tax department asks that you exercise discretion, but that doesn't mean that you must risk drowning."

I lowered my head in embarrassment. There was no sense challenging Marvin. Marvin knows his stuff.

Anyway, that's the plan—paint oceans. And be sure you find someone to buy your oceans so that you can establish some relationship between the income and the expense. I don't think one painting sold to your mother-in-law will do it.

Number six is terrific. Marvin at his best. A little wild, perhaps; a trifle borderline: *Travel on the cruise ship with Marvin and take his tax course.* Marvin says that investment aids are deductible. I think that means that if you have a lot of money in the stock market, or even a little money and dwindling rapidly, you are entitled to deduct subscriptions to investment journals. Marvin also says that tax advice is deductible. If you have a tax problem and call your accountant and the accountant sends you a bill, that's deductible. So Marvin says that *he* is deductible also. After all, he argues, his course aboard ship provides important tax information that is essential to proper tax management plans. Since this lecture series is available nowhere else, you must take the cruise to get it. Conclusion: Marvin is deductible. Ponder that one for a while.

Thus ended Marvin's six ideas for writing off your cruise—all of them outrageous; all of them exciting; all of them creative. Some of them, he says, are just for fun, others could make you rich, and some could get you in a whole lot of trouble. All in all, they sound adventurous to me: wine merchant, artist, entrepreneur. A new life, full of romance and intrigue. Cannes, St. Thomas, Casablanca, Tahiti. I'm going, Marvin, I'm going. Even if I *can't* deduct it.

Getting Lost

I thought it might be a good idea to write about how to avoid getting lost. So I started to think about the times when I *was* lost, and as I thought about them I realized that they were the best times. It is a curious notion, but one of the most interesting things to do in the cities of Europe is to get lost.

There are, I suppose, two reservations. The first is that once lost you will not be found. You can solve that problem by stuffing a map in your pocket. Getting lost does not mean that when the sun goes down you must stay lost.

The other problem is wandering into dangerous sections. This is a problem that frightens urban Americans more than it should. We relate it to our own cities, but Rome is different from Detroit. There is an area of Rome that is moderately dangerous (some sections of the Trastevere), but *trastevere* means "across the river," and nobody crosses a river without being aware of it.

It is important to mention these reservations, because if you get lost and you are anxious to get found, the whole idea has no value. You must relax; you must meander; you must have no purpose or direction except to slide into the rhythm and spirit of the city.

And suddenly you are there. Once you've untracked yourself from the boulevards and avenues, from the jewelry shops and the fine leather goods stores, the city gently and subtly changes color. The stores become furniture shops and bakeries. Not bakeries selling the elegant swirled pastries, but bakeries selling crusty bread and rolls. And you walk by a pasta shop where the proprietor is pressing out the pasta into sheets, passing it through rollers that were once used to press the water out of clothing before there were dryers.

The city has changed. You have wandered out of the areas that support the tourist business and into the areas that support the life of the city. There are butcher shops, an outdoor market, a shoe shop with prices one-third as high as on the boulevards. The smells and the sounds of the city are here. Wash is hung out, children are crying, old men sit around in circles and smoke, women haggle in the shops. School breaks, and a rush of laughing, pushing ten-year-olds, dressed in white blouses and shirts with orange ties, dash across your path. You enter a large square and the children are playing take-a-giant-step and the local version of ring-a-leevio. Here is the pulsebeat of the city—the part of Lisbon that doesn't care if there are tourists around, the rare section of London or Copenhagen that supports the everyday life of the city.

Here you are a stranger but not a tourist. As unusual as the people may be to you, you are to them. When you walk into their shops, whether you buy or not, they are interested. They do not, as on the grand boulevards, spend half their day talking to foreign tourists. You are, if you can possibly imagine this, an event in their lives.

I always wander into these little shops and ask for directions. I ask not to find out where I am, but because I can't think of another way of starting a simple conversation. They give you directions and then say, "American?" You answer, "From New York." And suddenly there is language and warmth. They have a nephew in New York.

"What does he do?"

"*Studente.*"

"What do *you* do?" they ask.

"Clothing for little girls."

Actually I *look* for clothing shops, because I can begin a conversation without asking for directions. I can say that I'm manufacturing clothing in America and that I am interested in seeing what they sell here. They are delighted and ask dozens of questions. "How much would this blouse cost in America?" "How much does a factory worker earn?"

Don't ever be frightened by the language barrier. It's more fun if you can speak a little of the language, but there is no question that you can get by without it. There is a universal language that binds people in a small shop. You may not know the word for "dress," but the shopkeeper does, because over the years, in any foreign country, even outside of the tourist routes, the shopkeeper has learned how to say "dress" in five languages. After all, that's what he sells. That is what his world is all about.

The shops along the tourist routes are fascinating—the Stroget in Copenhagen, St. Mark's Square in Venice, Piccadilly Circus in London—but they are not where the city breathes. It is those sections where you are lost that are the marrow of the city.

When you are lost, and comfortably lost, your intellect relaxes and your senses take over. You hear and see and smell more of the city because you are not going anywhere, not involved with time, and not a part of a tour or group. There is no plan, no arrangement to things. So you forget north and south, and whether the Eiffel Tower is on your left or right. You stand in the city as you might stand in the woods, and the city seeps in and penetrates.

You come to sense the language—the pure sound of it, the melody. You develop an innate feeling for the people, for their dress, their color, their mannerisms. You even come to know the courtesy or the arrogance, the warmth or the reserve.

It's five o'clock and you return to the mainstream, but you have come away with a new sense of things—impossible to find on the Champs-Élysées or the Via Veneto.

You come away feeling the Italianness or the Swedishness of the people. And you have the feeling that if you were dropped down from the sky into that country, you would still know—from the sounds of the throat and the slick of the hair, from the waving of the arms and the grain of the skin—exactly where you were.

Remembering the Unrememberable

It's kind of a silly idea, and I mention it with some hesitation, but we keep lists. By "we" I mean the five members of our family, and by "lists" I mean that we record all the museums or restaurants that we have visited and then we rate them. It is sort of the Academy Awards of travel.

I find, when I try seven different restaurants in a city, that my memory blurs, and a week after I have left the city all the restaurants are just names. I find in particular, when I visit a country like France or Italy, that my mind will carry only so much of the great art. After a week I can no longer picture the Botticellis in the Uffizi, the Giottos in Padua, or the Caravaggios in Rome. It is a problem that we all have when we visit a museum—our minds will retain perhaps a dozen major works. After that we can no longer absorb, and furthermore, the first twelve begin to blur.

A rating system solves this problem. In order to rate works of art, you must constantly bring them forward as mental images. In retrieving them from your memory bank, back and forth, they become familiar. It sounds juvenile, but it does work. It works particularly well when you travel with children.

In Italy, aware that we were being inundated with overpowering paintings and sculpture, we set in motion the rating system. We waited until the fifth or sixth day of the trip and then we listed—recalling as we listed—some of the major works of art that we had seen. A single painting or sculpture may be considered a work of art. A church may be so considered. A part of a church, such as the doors of the Duomo in Florence, may be considered. The tile floor of the Cathedral of St. Mark in Venice is a candidate.

When the list was complete we voted, assigning positions from one to ten for each work.

There was a good deal of discussion and argument about this, and consequently a good deal of recollection. Rita and I tended to rate the creators of the Renaissance, Giotto and Duccio, above the High Renaissance school of Raphael, Leonardo, and Michelangelo. Our three children thought otherwise. What do children know?

The important thing is that the list was established. And then—and this is the exciting part—on the seventh day we visited Siena to see the collection of Duccios in the Opera del Duomo. Magnificent. But where will it go on the list? Will it slide into fourth place ahead of the Botticelli *Primavera* in the Uffizi? "Of course," cry the parents. "Never!" respond the children. And the debate rages on.

I thought it remarkable that my children were willing to discuss Duccio *at all*. But what happens is that Duccio becomes fun. And while the pure aesthetics of line and perspective are given less time than the position on the rating chart, I'll settle for that.

I would be hard pressed to argue with someone who scoffed and called it a silly game, who said that we should appreciate the painting for its own value. He's right, of course, but do not presume that the rating chart prevents that. On the contrary, it allows it, because it provides the essential factor of anchoring the painting in our memory.

So the purist approach of "the painting for its own sake" is valid, certainly. But see if your fifteen-year-old can remember, after two weeks of museums and church frescoes, what a Duccio looks like.

Our chart of paintings and sculpture in Italy was posted in our home when we returned, and the debate continued. A dissident voice would indicate with a red arrow that the Duccios belonged in ninth place instead of third. Another arrow elevated Michelangelo's *David* from eighth to fourth.

The amazing thing is that three teenagers, only moderately interested in art, and with tastes turning more toward Monet and van Gogh, can still recollect with clarity the Masaccios in the Brancacci Chapel, or the incredibly beautiful Simone Martini in the Uffizi. Our list? Well O.K., here it is:

1. The Sistine Chapel in Rome.
2. The Caravaggio paintings in the Church of San Luigi dei Francesi, in Rome.

3. The Duccio paintings in the Opera del Duomo, in Siena.
4. The Botticelli Room in the Uffizi, in Florence.
5. The Pinturicchio frescoes in the Libreria Piccolomini, in Siena.
6. The Giotto frescoes in the Scrovegni Chapel, in Padua.
7. The Duomo, in Florence.
8. Michelangelo's *David*, in Florence.
9. The Raphael Rooms in the Vatican Museum, in Rome.
10. The Simone Martini *Annunciation* in the Uffizi, in Florence.

Our list is neither scholarly nor defendable, but these are nevertheless the works of Italian art that we loved best. There is much that we missed. There is much that we didn't understand or appreciate. But these ten works, painstakingly narrowed from a list of thirty, we remember clearly. And we are likely to remember them for a long time.

Beware of Aero!

The mark of the truly sophisticated traveler is not dinner at Taillevent, in Paris. Anyone with seventy-five bucks can negotiate dinner at Taillevent. Nor is it riding a motor scooter along the Via Veneto in Rome. It takes no skill to crack up a Vespa in the insane Italian traffic. The test of the sophisticated traveler—the truly liberated, spirited, courageous traveler—comes on the beaches of Denmark, where they bathe nude.

Recognizing this, and anxious to be included among the international set, we planned to visit Copenhagen. The challenge was at hand.

I can struggle my way through Taillevent, and I have logged some Vespa miles around the streets of Europe, but nude bathing is quite another matter. My friends, recognizing my growing anxiety, were understanding and supportive.

"Well, since you're going to Denmark, I guess you'll come back and tell us all about nude bathing."

It was almost enough to call off the trip.

But Rita persisted and would hear nothing of Disneyland or Atlantic City, so we packed our bags for Copenhagen. I immediately developed a full-blown case of asthma and insisted upon a dry inland route.

Let me clarify a misconception about bathing in Scandinavia. Not everybody bathes nude. In fact, on the main beaches hardly anybody bathes nude. The distinction is this: On most beaches of the world people will arrive with a bathing suit on underneath their clothing. The Danes don't bother. So you will often see bathers changing into their suits, casual and relaxed, and there will be that moment of anxiety when they are neither dressed for the water nor dressed for the land.

The anxiety is not their anxiety, but mine. I always had my magazine ready. Here we were, 200 bathers standing around, with maybe three or four changing clothes. Everybody is watching the water or watching the sun, or even watching the nude bathers. One person is intently reading the *Atlantic Monthly.*

Denmark includes three main bodies of land, Zealand, Funen, and Jutland. Ninety percent of the travelers never get beyond Zealand, which includes the city of Copenhagen and is the most interesting and alive of the three areas. It is also the area that has the least nude bathing, because in season there are probably more tourists than Danes in Zealand. The tourists are standing around the beaches waiting for everybody to go bathing in the nude, and all they observe is other tourists observing them. So, needless to say, I was safe in Zealand.

Our trip called for visiting all three areas, and after a week in and around Copenhagen we headed for Funen, a smaller area to the west. We stayed there for three days, and on one of those days we took a ferry to Aero, a small island to the south.

Why Aero? I don't know. Probably someone said it was a place where tourists never visit. That attracts me every time. I know I can come back to New York and impress everyone. There's nothing like visiting a place that nobody has ever been to.

Let me say this to the travelers of the world—let me warn both the brave and the timid: *Beware of Aero.*

Aero *is* a place where very few tourists visit, and the reason is that there's nothing much to do on the island. The main activity seems to be swimming, so we drove the fifteen-mile length of the island and then pulled off the road at a beach near the far end. By now I had survived the beaches of Copenhagen, and I pointed out to Rita with considerable arrogance that there was nothing going on along this country's coastline that I couldn't handle. (I said this while clutching tightly my copy of the *Atlantic Monthly.*)

We walked onto the beach. There were perhaps thirty bathers—they were all nude.

I turned back to the car, but Rita wouldn't let me. "There's no sign that reads you *must* bathe nude," she said.

"O.K.," I said, "I'll stay, but hand me my bathrobe. I'm going to change into my bathing suit."

"You're wearing your bathing suit under your chinos," she said.

"Hand me my bathrobe anyway," I said. "It's a little chilly on the beach."

I stripped down to my bathing suit (Rita didn't do any better), hid behind my magazine, and surveyed the situation. Naked bodies everywhere, swimming, sunning, jumping around. Sodom and Gomorrah.

It pains me to confess this, because it is not the way I prefer to see myself. In my Walter Mitty life I am the adventurous and sophisticated traveler. I daydream discussing Bronzino and Pontormo with the curator of the Uffizi in Florence. He remarks at my discriminating taste, and we bow to each other once or twice.

In Paris I am at Tour d'Argent, where I am recognized by the sommelier. He hurries to my table to ask whether I agree that the '66 Médocs are maturing better than the '64s. We chat about Château Talbot and Cos d'Estournel, reminiscing about past bottles enjoyed, the year, and the particular character.

In Stockholm I dream myself with the American ambassador, drinking aquavit and toasting, "Skoal." He asks about inflation, and how I feel about gold futures.

In short, my fantasies have no boundaries. When in Rome, I do as the Romans.

But that has to mean, when in Denmark, do as the Danes, and the Danes often bathe nude. In my Walter Mitty life I have swashbuckled my way through all obstacles. Why can't I handle this?

I know why, actually. You can *learn* about Château Talbot 1966, and Bronzino and Pontormo. They are not things that you are, but facts that you acquire. What you are has to do with the way you grew up, and I grew up on the beaches of Coney Island and Atlantic City. I'm Brooklyn born and bred, and condemned to the Brooklyn morality forever.

So there I am, standing on a beach in some far corner of the world, and oh my God, nobody has any clothes on. I really don't have a Walter Mitty self to deal with this.

"Let's get out of here," I tell Rita. "Maybe we'll come back tomorrow."

But we don't leave, because Rita's Walter Mitty is less embarrassed than mine, so I gird myself for adventures-to-come. And just over the top edge of my magazine I spot a couple on a blanket about ten yards from ours. They are nude, of course, so I order Rita to look in another direction. (There's no hope for me, is there?) ·

I peer innocently over my screen, and in a moment the young lady rises from her towel and begins to rub herself with suntan oil. Well, for goodness sakes, the sun was very strong!

She's about five-foot eight and extremely lovely, and she must be very susceptible to sunburn, because she isn't missing any areas. And now she's finished—oh no, she's not. There are some areas that she can't reach, so her boyfriend is kindly going to reach them for her.

I can't stand much of this; maybe I'll make a break for the car. On the other hand, maybe I won't.

None of this is escaping Rita, who has paid no attention whatever to my restrictions on her field of vision. It is only fair to point out that even if she had looked in another direction, there is no telling what she might have seen.

"Let's get out of here," I repeated.

"How come you didn't suggest that when she *started* to oil herself?" Rita asked.

"Because I didn't want to embarrass her," I lied.

But the truth was, I didn't belong. It was a beach for nude bathing, for people entirely comfortable with nudity, not for an uptight New Yorker with a *Good Housekeeping* mentality. Alas, I'll never make it with the international set.

I do often think about the young lady and the suntan oil, although I can't tell you what I think, or this book will find its way into the porno shops. It did occur to me that if the advertising agency that handles Sea & Ski could get a few shots of that scene on the island of Aero, it would sell a whole lot of suntan lotion.

How to Pronounce "Copenhagen"

For months, before we left for Denmark, friends and world travelers cautioned us about the one thing we *must get right* in Copenhagen.

Naturally I got very excited when I heard this, because I figured it had something to do with sex. After all, everything is out in the open in Denmark, so it must be some protocol like: Don't touch it if it's still light out.

Alas, it wasn't that at all. It concerns how you pronounce "Copenhagen."

Don't laugh at this, because it is absolutely true. Any number of people have said quite seriously:

"You're going to Denmark? I'll give you one important piece of advice. Never say 'CopenHAHgen,' say 'CopenHAYgen.' "

And as you turn away to make a stab at the hors d'oeuvres tray, they say:

"This is a serious matter. If you say 'CopenHAHgen' you will offend the Danes. 'CopenHAHgen' is what the Germans said during the War, and the Danes still resent it."

Well now, this *is* a serious matter. Already I'm a war criminal. So I immediately set out to train myself to say "CopenHAYgen," automatically.

This is not so easy. I naturally say "CopenHAHgen," since that's what Danny Kaye said when he was Hans Christian Andersen.

About a week before we left I was still saying it wrong, and I was getting pretty worried about it.

"How do you feel about going to Brussels?" I asked Rita.

"Why that's a wonderful idea for next year . . . "

"For this year."

"What are you talking about? We're leaving next week."

"I don't think I can go. I still can't get 'CopenHAYgen' right."

"Oh, that? That's just silliness. What do you think will happen? They'll take our passports away?"

Women never have a sense of international crisis. "An incident like this started World War I," I said.

"O.K., we'll go to Brussels. *You* call the travel agent and change all the plans."

So we went to Copenhagen.

I studied hard all that week, and I was finally getting it toward the end. Of course, other things suffered. I hadn't time to learn the currency, or simple words like "thank you" and "please." But I was getting "Copenhagen."

And when we landed and got our luggage into a cab, I shouted, "CopenHAYgen."

The driver looked at me strangely.

I thought maybe I didn't emphasize it enough, so I shouted "CopenHAYgen" again, a little louder on the "HAY" part.

I think he got it. It may have been because there was hardly anything else that two American tourists could have been saying.

"*Jah, København*," he said politely.

It didn't sound like "CopenHAYgen" to me. It sounded like "KURBENHOWN."

As we drove toward the city a thought suddenly hit me—why didn't Danny Kaye say "CopenHAYgen"? I mean if the Danes were so concerned about it, it seems that Hollywood would have Danny Kaye say it the right way.

So I asked the cab driver how the Danes preferred it pronounced.

"Well," he said, "the Germans say 'CopenHAHgen.'" (I gave Rita a knowing glance.) "And the Americans and English say 'CopenHAYgen.' But the Danes have no preference."

"No preference! That can't be. Every American tourist says the Danes prefer 'CopenHAYgen.'"

"There are some things that American tourists are wrong about," he said.

I went on to tell him about the reasons for this—about the Germans and World War II—but he had never heard of it. "The War was forty years ago," he said.

Well, all right, maybe he hadn't heard of it. But all those American tourists can't be wrong. So I asked the next Dane I met, the owner of a jewelry shop. He hadn't heard of it either.

Rita said that maybe we had to ask an older citizen, someone more likely to relate to the War. We did. He related to the War, but had no preference about "Copenhagen."

I continued to ask around. I must have asked twenty people. Not one of them had a preference, or had ever heard of another Dane who did have a preference. They all politely scoffed at the World War II story.

A hotel manager said, "I think most Danes, when they are speaking English or German, say 'CopenHAHgen.' That's probably because it sounds a little closer to *København* in Danish. But nobody has a preference—unless you care to pronounce it 'KURBENHOWN,' the way the Danes do."

Actually, that's not a bad idea.

The Indispensable Dark Blue Suit

In Europe, particularly in the countries that border on the Mediterranean, there is a strict hierarchy of social station and class strata. Americans, raised in the melting pot of the world, don't understand it at all. In Portugal or Greece there will be seven women standing in line in a bakeshop and the seventh will move up to the front. Her aggression is not contested; she is the wife of the town merchant or the doctor. The others are wives of the fishermen. It is understood that she takes her rightful place in the order of things.

There is an American woman, studying art in Rome, who always gets dressed up to go shopping. In the winter she wears her fur coat to the bakery. The rationale? To establish herself in the hierarchy. She claims that when she is well dressed people will not move in front of her in the line, and if there is no line, the shopkeeper will quickly single her out and take her order. She also claims that if she is not well dressed she can wave her arms at the shopkeeper and he will look right through her. She concedes that the system is preposterous, but argues that she has only so many hours to do her shopping.

If you watch the Europeans carefully you will notice this respect for position. In the restaurants and the hotels, where you can watch the captain and the waiter and the busboy, you will observe that each knows exactly where he fits. It is an innate, almost devout regard for social strata. Their voices, their dress, and their postures reflect precisely the order of things. And it is not only that they observe rank—Americans *observe* rank—but Europeans respect and honor rank. And it is not so much that they observe rank on the production line and then go home to the corner bar where everybody is the same as everybody else. Rank is always: on the job, in the bar, waiting in line, getting served in a restaurant. And Europeans always dress according to rank. An executive would consider it demeaning to be seen without his conservative blue suit and tie. The laborer does not dare to pretend to such position, and wears his gray cardigan sweater.

The American traveler, oblivious to these class strata, walks into a restaurant, a shop, or a travel agency wearing an open-collar print shirt, his black-watch plaid slacks, and maybe a comfortable, loose-fitting sport jacket. Why not? He's on vacation. In America, this is what you wear when you are on vacation.

He enters a restaurant, and behind him are two other American tourists wearing suits and ties. The proprietor walks right by him and offers the next table to the gentleman behind him, and then walks right by him again when the second table appears. Finally he is seated, close to the kitchen door perhaps. An affront? Not really. It is just the proprietor observing the order of things. Remember, it's their country.

The same tourist, wearing the same print sport shirt, finds himself at the airport, flying from Lisbon to Madrid. Everybody is crowded around the counter; there is some confusion. Everyone is getting waited on ahead of him. Finally a serious problem develops: The flight is overbooked. He has a ticket and he wants to see a supervisor, but nobody will listen. The dignified gentleman to his right approaches the counter; people move out of his way. He places his ticket on the counter with a flourish, stands erect, and fairly paralyzes the clerk with a cold stare. His ticket is accepted. Outrage! Yes, it is, but meanwhile he is on the flight and the open-collar sport shirt is not.

In Europe, dress commands attention. Of course it's silly. Of course it's irrational. But do you want to be rational or do you want to get on the flight? I have found, invariably, that I am treated with respect when I wear my dark blue suit and conservative tie and I am treated casually when I wear my print shirt and sport jacket. And when I wear my print shirt without my sport jacket I'm ignored altogether.

Since I'm not interested in altering the social strata of a continent, I wear my suit and tie. When I travel I *absolutely* wear my suit and tie because the consequences of being ignored when you travel could be that the train leaves and you don't. When I go to a restaurant I wear my suit and tie because I prefer to sit near the window and away from the swinging doors. Even when I walk around the city I try to look respectable, because I never know when I will walk into a jewelry shop or a leather-goods store.

Rita does exactly the same thing, because obviously the same rule applies. She leaves her Acapulco outfits at home and brings a simple dress or a conservative pants suit. How dull, you say? Perhaps so, but this is not a fashion show or a first night. The purpose of bringing clothes, it seems to me, is to be comfortable and appropriate.

If I had to name one travel suggestion that is essential, this is it. And Americans invariably ignore it, ultimately to their distress and discomfort. When we travel, we are in strange lands, or at least they are strange to us, as New York and Chicago would be strange to the Europeans. Strange lands have strange customs, and the customs are centuries old and immutable.

In Europe the custom is, dress according to your station. We may not agree, but it would help to understand.

A Guide to Guides

"My last client was Ted Kennedy," says my guide. "He sat right there, in your seat. You know Teddy, don't you?"

I shift a bit, embarrassed to be occupying so distinguished a seat. "Well, not exactly," I respond.

"I took Ted all around London. I guess I'll take you on the same tour."

And so, in two minutes of conversation, I have once again been intimidated by my guide. I have been told where I want to go and relegated to second-class citizenship. This seems to be my predictable experience.

The "Ted Kennedy guide" is only one of many; my guides fall into four categories:

1. THE CONNOISSEUR. It doesn't matter if we are not interested in buying—and we are not—there are always four shops that we have to see.

We're in Florence, and as soon as we enter the car or limousine, the conversation turns to buying things. Are we interested in Florentine gold or hand-tooled leather? No, actually we're not. Well, that means instead of visiting four shops we have to visit only two. Can't we skip that part altogether? Why certainly, we can skip it altogether except for just a little peek in the window. After all, we're going to be right there anyway.

So immediately the air gets tense, because we know that the guide is going to steer us along the commerce route. Of course it won't seem that way. There will be the Uffizi Gallery, and around the corner will just happen to be "the jewelry shop that tourists never get to—that requires a special invitation—where the prices are 50% off."

If we're assertive and put our foot down, then the driver will approach it differently. Surely we want to see how Florentine gold is crafted. Nothing to buy—just a working shop turning out bracelets and pendants according to the traditions of the Renaissance artisans. The Old World preserved—a chance to see it before they tear it down. The Florence of Leonardo and Michelangelo.

Well yes, we would like to see that, and soon we enter the back door of the shop, where our guide and the floor manager exchange glances. We are taken along a row of metal workers who are doing some interesting things, but of course we're not allowed to walk slowly enough to watch them. We can't even enjoy the workmanship, because there is that tension, that tightening of the stomach, that tells us the owner of the shop will soon introduce himself, and will suggest—because he can see that we are people of discriminating taste—that there are some incredible pieces in his private office. It will take only a moment, of course. "I understand," he says, "you are not here to shop for jewelry."

Alas, how to refuse him? It's so painful. So we follow him to his private office, where the velvet-lined boxes appear. And the jewelry is very nice, but we're in Florence, and we can buy jewelry in New York or Chicago. What we can't do in New York or Chicago is see the priceless paintings in the Uffizi.

We escape, with appropriate gestures of goodwill, and of course we're fuming at our guide, and I guess at our own gullibility. But fighting with guides is not my idea of a restful vacation, so we're on our way.

Wait—we're not on our way; it's lunchtime. And right down the block, our guide advises, is a restaurant that serves the best scallopini in Florence. But we're wiser now, so we *tell* the guide where we want to have lunch. A lovely spot, he agrees, but on the other side of Florence, and impossible to work into the itinerary he has planned for us. Try this place, he urges; he took a couple from New York, and they raved about it. We open our restaurant guide. One star. Well, at least it's listed.

We go inside—*buon giornos* all around, but a noticeable coolness between the guide and the maître d'. Don't they know each other? Of course they do; the bloodlines run back three generations. But reserve is called for, and the guide bows out, later to return for his reward. We settle down to lunch, accompanied by a

full bottle of Valpolicella to drown the pain. I've been hustled again.

2. THE MONA LISA GUIDE. We're at the Louvre, in Paris, and it's a race to the *Mona Lisa*. We zip past Courbet and Delacroix. "Wait a minute!" my subconscious screams. "I want to see these." But no, it's a quarter-mile sprint to the *Mona Lisa*, which is certainly important, but there are a dozen other paintings that are just as important.

It's the mentality that bothers me, and perhaps I'm unfair. I suppose countless tourists have asked to see the *Mona Lisa*, and the guide is simply responding to what he thinks we want. But isn't there room for a word about Titian or Giorgione? Isn't there an argument for beginning without a predisposed, almost religious devotion to one painting?

We move on to the Jeu de Paume, and what do we find? A word about the forerunners of Impressionism? A comparison, however basic, between Pissarro and Monet? No, of course not. The first thing we hear about is how van Gogh cut off his ear. And it's not the fact, but the telling of it that bothers me. We are first gathered close together, like a family about to hear a last will and testament. Then there is the moment of silence while the audience is surveyed. Then that self-satisfied smile, hands clasped in front of him, and finally the benediction. "Did you know that van Gogh cut off his ear?"

"Really?" I reply, with predictable bravado.

"Is that so?" says Rita, just as courageous.

And we proceed to the Eiffel Tower.

There are probably a number of reasonably interesting things about the Eiffel Tower. For example, why was such a strange structure built? But those are not the things I'm going to hear. I'm going to hear about the daredevils and acrobats who have been killed trying to scale the beams or fly through the arches. Actually, that's not exactly boring, but by now I've turned sour. By now I'm like the theatergoer who has watched an actor stumble over his lines for two acts. He can be brilliant in the third act and it will not matter. He can't recover, because I've become uncomfortable watching him.

And let me not limit myself to guides overseas, because I hired a guide in New York recently—I had out-of-town guests—and when we arrived downtown at the Twin Towers he told the story of how a guy walked a tightrope across them. It's a good story, but that's all he told.

3. THE LET'S-BE-PALS GUIDE. I suppose I'm stuffy about things like this, but instant friendship is not what I want from my guide. It therefore follows, doesn't it, that every guide I get reveals the most personal and intimate circumstances of his home life not more than five minutes after we've met. Generally the circumstances suggest a home life of less than ideal conditions, coupled with certain satellite social arrangements that I am expected to understand and condone.

I know whether I have a guide or a pal within the first minute. If he starts calling me Lenny, I don't have a guide. Some may suggest that what you are called depends upon what you allow yourself to be called. I am genuinely impressed by travelers who have such tight control of the situation. I presume that when they are called Lenny, they reply rather sternly, "Mr. Bernstein would be preferable." I admire their bravery, and I admit outright that my defenses hold no such armor.

Lenny is not the worst thing to be called. It's what follows that creates the problem. Travelers called Mr. Bernstein get to hear about the Colosseum; travelers called Lenny get to hear about the guide's sex life. I might point out that I am now an expert on this subject.

I think guides must get understandably bored talking about the Colosseum (as do most of their listeners) and prefer, if allowed, to discuss more spicy topics. Once into these areas, they are never out. Everything reminds them of some personal matter. A Rubens painting, especially a fleshy Rubens painting, calls to mind a wife or a girlfriend. A painting of a child will elicit a group portrait of the family, complete with second and third cousins. In front of Manet's nude *Olympia*, I get a light elbow in the ribs and a little nod. And then, "How do you say in America? The real stuff?"

The guide also delights in telling you about the previous couple. If they made love in the backseat, he tells. If they fought all day, he tells.

"Hey, Lenny, I had this couple before you. You know what they do all day?"

"No. What?"

"They fight. All day long they fight. As soon as they get in the car, I ask where do they want to go. He says the Vatican. She says the Colosseum. For half an hour we don't go anywhere. You know what she finally calls him?"

"No, I don't, but maybe we could skip that part."

4. THE SELECT CLIENTELE GUIDE. Somehow, every guide I get has just finished driving around Richard Burton. I wish Burton would stop following me around the world because it's damn annoying. And furthermore, it's not only that Burton has come before me, but that Redford is coming after. I'm like the in-between; the comic relief, the short between two feature movies.

Naturally I'm impressed to know that Richard Burton has just sat in this very same seat, but immediately I am the slave in the game of one-upmanship.

"I'll take you to the same places I took Burton," he says.

What's a guy to say to that?

Sometimes the select clientele guide does not come right out and say that he just finished driving around Richard Burton. He plays the Celebrity Mystery Game. "Guess who I just had in my limousine?"

This evolves into a form of Twenty Questions, in which I am not allowed to know who the Mystery Guest is without the appropriate initiation. Here I am, spending a fortune to drive around Rome, and I'm playing guessing games. Well, it's not really as bad as that, but I'm not far off the mark.

The most unpleasant aspect of the guide who has (or says he has) just driven around Richard Burton, is that Burton and the guide are now obviously best friends. Consequently, I am treated to gentle innuendos about Burton's private life. "You know, Richard takes a nip now and then." Since I don't know anyone who doesn't take a nip now and then—usually now—I hardly regard this as a bit of information likely to highlight my trip.

You are entitled to ask how I find my way around a strange city, since I have become so disillusioned with the professional guides. And let me be clear about this; I wish I *could* use a guide, because I have no better approach.

But I do have an idea that is delightful when it works, and since some travelers may also be unlucky with guides, maybe the idea is worth trying.

I go straight to the university and ask for a student or a professor who would like to show us around the city. Within an hour a rather good-looking young man enters the office, introduces himself as an associate professor of Renaissance art, and says he would be happy to introduce us to Florence or Rome, although we must understand that he is not a professional guide.

He's bright and fresh. His English is good enough and his concepts are imaginative, so we proceed to see the city through new eyes. We are captivated by his enthusiasm and his intellect. It is so different from that tired, bored, I've-done-it-all-before approach of the professional guide.

When I'm in Rome I call the American Academy, Via Masina 5, which houses American art students and practicing artists working and studying in Rome. Actually I write in advance, because by now I have a few names, but I have no doubt that if I arrived in Rome tomorrow I could call the Academy and be directed to someone who would be happy to guide me through the Sistine Chapel.

Of course it doesn't always work out. Not every student at the Academy or professor at the university is interesting. But there is at least the possibility of excitement, and it is always better than getting a guide from the concierge at the hotel.

And for those of us who follow in the footsteps of Ted Kennedy and Richard Burton, it is essential.

Traveling as Leonard Bernstein

In my life there are two Leonard Bernsteins; there's me and there's him. Actually, there's not a lot of me, and an awful lot of him.

It all started in 1943. Up to then there was only me. I was twelve, and in seventh grade at P.S. 193 in Brooklyn. On the Sunday afternoon of November 14, Bruno Walter, the guest conductor of the New York Philharmonic, became suddenly ill, and a young, virtually unknown understudy was called to take his place. The performance was brilliant, and the following day the newspapers headlined the story across America. The young conductor was Leonard Bernstein.

On Monday morning I took my seat in class; first row, third seat, right next to the bulletin board. I knew nothing of events at the New York Philharmonic, but our teacher, Mrs. Schrader, did; the bulletin board was a collage of headlines and photos. It was difficult for a twelve-year-old to entirely understand. Someone with the same name as me was famous.

It was customary for Mrs. Schrader to post and then discuss the news events of the day. As she began to discuss Leonard Bernstein, thirty heads turned toward me and smiled. Not bad, so far.

Mrs. Schrader was ecstatic about the performance. She explained the various character traits that were demonstrated: initiative, dedication, perseverence, discipline. And then she turned to me (I remember this very clearly) and said:

"What are *you* going to do, Leonard?"

I think it is a credit to the Leonard Bernstein who was twelve, that he survived this event and was graduated from public school. But that was hardly to be the end of comparisons, jokes, and mistaken identities. Bernstein climbed to the top of the world of music, and he became one of the best-known names in the United

States—in the world. It was impossible to go anywhere without someone remarking about my name.

Let me say this: If you have to get stuck with a name, there is none better than "Leonard Bernstein." There is nobody more respected, more accomplished, more honored. It is almost impossible to make a nasty remark about him. He simply soars above it. So that when I telephone an airline or a hotel to make a reservation, triggering an inevitably familiar dialogue, the jokes may be stale, but they don't hurt.

You probably think it's exciting to travel as Leonard Bernstein. You probably think I get the best hotel accommodations, fifth-row-center at the theaters, and the champagne and caviar treatment on Pan Am. Actually, I could get all those things if I reserved in the name of Leonard Bernstein, but then so could you if *you* reserved in the name of Leonard Bernstein. The problem would arise, not with the reservations, but when you showed up. Clearly they would be expecting someone else.

Ah, you say, but there's a difference. Leonard Bernstein is my real name. I have a right to reserve in my own name. You're correct about that, but legality is not the issue. The issue is promise and disappointment. When I show up, I'm just as much *not* Leonard Bernstein as you are. Do you think I can finesse the situation by explaining that Leonard Bernstein is my real name? Of course not. The more I explain, the worse it gets.

If I call Maxim's in Paris with a dinner reservation in the name of Leonard Bernstein, the red carpet will be rolled out. It matters not that the restaurant is booked solid; a table in the dress circle will magically appear. And who will be waiting at the door to greet the honored guest but the maître d' and the owner. Then I show up and say, "My name is Leonard Bernstein, and I have a dinner reservation at eight." I assure you it doesn't work. Napoleon at Waterloo didn't face such humiliation.

The same is true in hotels. If they receive a reservation in the name of Leonard Bernstein, they set aside the emperor's suite. When I show up and mention the reservation they assume I'm the advance party, sent ahead to be sure the windows are open and the hot water is running. I go up in the service elevator.

Which is not to say that it is never an advantage. When an airline, particularly the airline of a foreign country, receives a reservation in the name of Leonard Bernstein—tourist class—they get all confused. Maybe there's a slipup, they figure, and what-the-hell, they haven't got anybody sitting in first class anyway. Better to give away a little pâté and champagne than put Bernstein in the teeming masses of a 747. Ordinarily my arrival should straighten this out, but somehow it doesn't seem to. Either the check-in counter doesn't know the Bernstein profile, or their instructions are already irrevocable. In any case, I follow the carpet into first class.

If they challenge me, I'm always truthful, but if they ask, "Are you Leonard Bernstein?" they are not going to solve the dilemma. And if they ask, "Are you the *real* Leonard Bernstein?" they are *certainly* not going to solve the dilemma. If I'm not real, what am I?

But if they ask, "Are you the conductor?" or anything else reasonable, they are entitled to the truth.

All of this doesn't prevent me from approaching the counter with a particularly noble bearing and an air that intimidates. That's fair game. What is not fair game would be mentioning to Rita something about the first violinist. Obviously deceitful, lowbrow, and crass. I often think about it, though.

Even in moments when my intentions remain honorable, I get into trouble. I specifically caution travel agents to be certain to wire ahead that the Leonard Bernstein arriving is me and not him. Apparently the distinction of reserving for Leonard Bernstein is more than some agents can resist, especially since *they* don't have to show up. So there is always that moment of apprehension as I approach the reservations desk. I just have to hope that the agent played it straight.

Another unavoidable situation occurs when I am traveling in a more remote area where English is only hesitantly spoken. I call and make a reservation, usually in the name of L. Bernstein. If they insist on a first name I tell them, but I immediately launch a long-memorized and urgent appeal not to get the name confused; not to expect the conductor. It is possibly not the clearest of denials to someone who doesn't understand English very well, or Italian spoken with a Brooklyn accent, and we occasionally find ourselves with the top floor of the hotel all to ourselves. You might think that's a lovely idea, and you would be right—up until the moment the bill arrives.

And so, that marvelous name is not negotiable and not to be shared. It is protected by the surest armor that exists, the very distinction of the owner.

When you travel as Leonard Bernstein, you do not carry a magic key or an Aladdin's lamp to open the doors of the world. Rather, it's like a courier bearing a letter with the king's wax seal. It's an honor to carry, but it deserves special handling.

Visiting the Dark Continent

In the year 1871, Stanley traveled through darkest Africa in his search for Dr. Livingstone. Communications were almost nonexistent, supplies had to be backpacked, and hostile warrior tribes were a constant threat. A century later Americans travel overseas to France, Israel, and Japan, but their psychology is the same as Stanley's. When Americans travel overseas we assume we are visiting a Dark Continent.

The first time Rita and I went to Paris we were in a taxi, halfway to Kennedy Airport, when I realized I had forgotten my toothbrush. I told the driver to pull off the expressway at the next exit so I could find a drugstore and buy one. Rita, sitting right next to me, also recognized the danger: You don't go to Europe without a toothbrush. How are you going to brush your teeth? Of course it occurred to neither of us that twelve million toothbrushes are sold in Paris every year. After all, how do the French brush their teeth?

Our anxiety is caused by our failure to perceive that there is intelligent life overseas. Oh yes, we know there are people, but that knowledge is abstract; they are people on another planet. They don't shave, dress, or brush their teeth. We cannot envision that there is an everyday life in Europe—that people use safety pins and scissors, subways and buses, mouthwash and deodorant. We realize that there are stores, but they are stores selling Dior creations or Arpège. We do not imagine that there are department stores like Gimbel's or Sears that sell handkerchiefs and socks. Actually, we do not consider that the Frenchman *wears* socks. He remains, in our image, abstract, sans flesh and blood, an invisible man.

That is also the way we perceive *life* overseas. It has no pulse. People do not wake up and go to work, or fight with their spouses, or get toothaches. They exist, sort of, in limbo. Yes, we can see them—they are there. They serve dinner in the restaurants, and stand behind the reservations desk in hotels. But they do not have lives of their own.

It is curious, but true. We see life overseas only as it relates to our presence there. That there should be an everyday world of scraped knees and mortgage payments, of coffee breaks and Sunday comics, exceeds our field of vision.

So it is understandable that we have anxiety attacks as we leave the house. We run back inside four times, leaving the cab driver waiting while we check to be sure we packed our cuff links, aspirin, and alarm clock. And in the cab and on the plane, our minds race frantically back home. What did we forget? Something to read? A pen? Some Band-Aids?

Worst of all, we worry endlessly about instructions. Did we tell the children that we might be leaving Paris a day early? Did we tell them what to do if the plumber calls? And did we tell the stockbroker to sell Texaco if the price goes over sixty?

Would we worry quite as much if we traveled to Dallas? Of course not. We could telephone from Dallas. But Rome—we can't telephone from Rome. We're cut off. It does remotely occur to us that there is such a thing as a transatlantic phone call, but that's also an abstraction, something that is not done except in emergencies. And even then, it would be incredibly expensive, and we would have to wait around the hotel all day until the call got through. And after it got through, we wouldn't be able to hear anything at the other end. We are all Stanleys, visiting the Dark Continent.

It would never occur to us to call our stockbroker from Paris and tell him to sell Texaco, or to call our children and ask them how they are. It's part of our isolation complex, the same complex that prevents us from understanding that we can buy a toothbrush in Paris.

Yet, making a phone call from Europe is easier than buying a toothbrush and cheaper than buying a dinner. Isn't it worth a few dollars to find out how Grandma is feeling? More important, isn't it relaxing to know that if you are stranded on the Dark Continent, the communication lines are still open, and if you *do* forget something or get lonesome, or start to worry about the price of Texaco, all you have to do is pick up the phone?

Connections? Well, you can telephone Philadelphia from Paris as quickly as Philadelphia from Los Angeles. And count on hearing the voice at the other end just about as clearly as though you were in the same city.

You can buy everything in Europe except a hot dog, and that's only because the Europeans consider them uncivilized, a point you may agree with after you have tasted the cuisine of any country aside from England. You can buy anything, you can travel anywhere, and you can telephone easily. And you can therefore relax on the way over, and while you are there as well.

Why do we have the Dark Continent complex? I suspect it is because Americans have no concept of "foreign soil." That there is an everyday life cycle in Europe seems as remote as an everyday life cycle on Mars. We are, despite the amount of traveling that we do, an isolationist country in our concepts. Most of us live our lives among Americans and speak English exclusively, having no command of other languages. Nor do we often hear another language spoken. We are totally protected, even incubated, in the womb that is America. And while there is nothing wrong with that, it does make any exposure to an outside world alien and slightly threatening.

The Europeans are surrounded by travelers from many countries. Their lives are interwoven with those of foreigners, and other languages are commonplace. Consider that during the summer, in Paris and Copenhagen, Amsterdam and Madrid, there are almost as many foreigners in the city as natives. But in New York and Chicago, even today when Asians and Europeans are increasingly visiting the United States, you rarely are aware of the presence of a foreign tourist.

So the Europeans, exposed to foreigners, are familiar with the concept of people being on foreign soil. The American, unexposed, has precisely the opposite experience.

The predictable result is that we view a trip overseas as a safari through the jungle, and even after we are there and see that the people look pretty much the same as we do, we still hug the Via Veneto and the Champs-Élysées, and we make sure that we don't stray too far from the hotel.

Reflections

I would like to believe that within these pages, in between the far-out and whimsical schemes, some truth shines through. And the truth is: *Travel the way you want to.*

Every tourist is fairly battered with rules and regulations: You must visit the Colosseum. You must try these restaurants in Paris. You must buy leather in Florence. And it's not that the advice is bad, but it's stifling and uncreative. "Must" is an unfortunate word to take with you to Rome or Paris.

Europe is a time and a place for freedom. It's a time to sense yourself and to trust your instincts. Maybe you *are* the Colosseum type, which is, after all, not a bad type to be. But maybe you're not. Maybe you're the type to learn Italian and spend a day in the open market. How would you know? You've never been to Rome before. If you bring a list of rules and regulations, you'll travel the standard routes and never discover a thing about yourself.

Very likely you'll have a good time. It's difficult not to have a good time on vacation in the great cities of the world. We take our photographs, dine at the recommended restaurants, tour the city—and we're content. But we miss the moment of adventure. The moment is elusive; it is hidden behind decades of habit and convention.

And so, among these pages, are some good ideas, some bad ideas, some good sense and some nonsense. This is the way I like to travel. It might be the way *you* like to travel. There are new ideas and new paths waiting around every corner. They are unusual—yes—but perhaps we are also a little unusual.